W9-ADJ-105

GIFTED KIDS

Speak Out

Hundreds of kids ages 6-13 talk about school, friends, their families, and the future

James R. Delisle

free Spirit ®
PUBLISHING

FRANKLIN PIERCE COLLEGE
LIBRARY
RINDGE, NEW HAMPSHIRE

Copyright © 1987 by James R. Delisle

All rights reserved. No part of this book may be reproduced in any form except for brief reviews, without written permission of the publisher.

This paperback edition has been reprinted by arrangement with Walker and Company.

Library of Congress Cataloging-in-Publication Data

Gifted kids speak out

   Rev. ed. of: Gifted children speak out. 1984.
   Bibliography: p.
   1. Gifted children—Education—United States.
2. Gifted children—United States—Attitudes.
I. Delisle, James R. II. Gifted children speak out.
LC3993.9.G553 1987   371.95   87-25139
ISBN 0-915793-10-5

Printed in the United States of America

10 9 8 7 6 5 4 3 2

Edited by Judy Galbraith and Pamela Espeland
Cover and book design by MacLean & Tuminelly
Illustrations by Jackie Urbanovic

Free Spirit Publishing Inc.
400 First Avenue North, Suite 616
Minneapolis, MN 55401
(612) 338-2068

CURR
LC
3993.9
.G553
1987

**As before,
as always,
this book is
for Deb and Matt.**

Contents

Introduction

When I wanted to find out how kids felt about being gifted, I asked them. I made up questionnaires about the high points and hassles of being gifted and invited kids from ages 6 to 13 to respond.

More than 6,000 of them did. About 4,000 completed survey forms placed in The Association for the Gifted's *Update* publication, the MENSA Bulletin, and several newsletters for parents and teachers of gifted students. The other 2,000 or so completed surveys I handed out to gifted and talented teachers at local, state, and national conferences on gifted education.

I received responses from 37 states and U.S. territories, and from Canada, Germany, and Australia. Then came the hard part: I couldn't include all 6,000 in this book, so I had to choose among them.

I tried to select those that clearly expressed particular ideas. I also tried to present a range of responses that reflected the many other thoughts and feelings kids expressed. That's why some comments may seem illogical, vague, or a little strange. For example, one 13-year-old girl from Georgia wrote that she found out she was gifted at birth when "my doctor told my mother and my mother told me." It probably didn't happen in exactly that way—the story is probably a piece of family folklore—but she thinks it did, and that's important. (Also, comments like hers make for fun and interesting reading!)

After I had chosen the responses to put in this book, I still wasn't finished with it. I knew that you would want to read what other kids had to say about being gifted, but I also knew that this would start you thinking about how you would have answered the survey questions. That's why I added "Speak For Yourself" questions and activities at the end of each section. I wanted to give *you* a chance to speak out, too.

Some of the questions in the "Speak For Yourself" sections are best answered when you're all by yourself—in the privacy of your own mind. Others are meant to be discussed with others—friends, parents, teachers, counselors, or other adults. After reading the questions, try to answer them the best way you know how. Then consider whether or not you'd like to extend your thoughts about giftedness beyond just yourself.

Even though this book is printed and you're holding it in your hands, it *still* isn't finished. It doesn't include what *you* have to say.

But maybe the next edition will. In a way, this book is a continuation of my survey, and I hope someday to read *your* responses. I can only do that if you send them to me. Then maybe someday you'll read them in another book like this one. Who knows?

If you do decide to send me your responses, please write to me at this address:

Jim Delisle
401 White Hall
Kent State University
Kent, OH 44242

Meanwhile, I hope you have as much fun reading this book as I had putting it together. I also hope that it gives you a sense of community—a feeling that you're not alone. For many gifted kids, learning that there are others out there who think and feel the way they do comes as a big relief. Being gifted can get awfully lonely sometimes. It's nice to know that you're not the only person in the world who aces tests, learns faster than some other kids, thinks school can be boring, has parents who expect a lot, or, at times, finds it hard to get along with friends.

And it's nice to know that it's okay to feel good about being gifted, too. As one boy wrote, "I think it is special to be gifted and I never hide it."

Take Care,

Jim Delisle

CHAPTER 1

What Does It Mean To Be Gifted?

What Does It Mean to Be Gifted?

Being gifted means being able to comprehend and do things the average person does not know how to or does not want to know how to do. Being gifted also means having to do harder, more advanced work. To be frank and simple, being gifted is when you're more intelligent than most.

Girl, 10 Michigan

It means you can do lots of things without help from grown-ups.

Girl, 10, Arizona

...a brain that works overtime.

Girl, 12, Georgia

I think being gifted must mean being especially good in the arts as well as in the academic field. Some kids think that it just means being in an academically talented program, but a girl in *my* class with an IQ of 128 who is very good in art is automatically "not gifted" because you need an IQ of 130 to be in our gifted program. That's dumb.

Boy, 10, Connecticut

I know what the word gifted means, but from my point of view, I think most of the time it's used wrong. People tend to use the word gifted to describe a person good in school. Gifted *really* describes a person who is exceptionally good in anything, whether it's running or piano playing or reading. Everyone is gifted in some way.

Girl, 10, Indiana

I think it means being smart, having a wonderful imagination, and being different.

Girl, 12, Arkansas

I think smart and gifted are totally *different.* Being smart is just being able to answer questions and answer dates. Being gifted means you have an imagination and spirit and you are able to think creatively.

Girl, 10, Ohio

It means you are original and have good leadership qualities.

Girl, 12, Georgia

I think being gifted means having a special gift from God. I feel that if you are gifted, you are on earth to fulfill a need that (maybe) other people can't fulfill.

Girl, 12, Arkansas

Gifted is *definitely not,* in my mind, someone who is just a straight A student, though that might be one of the criteria. You must have that extra bit more of motivation that most kids don't have. You must be able to grasp complicated concepts and ideas easily and you must be responsible. Giftedness may not be something you always cherish, for it's a burden in many ways. But, being gifted, I find I have that urge to learn.

Boy, 12, Michigan

A gifted child is one who will explore new things, a child who will seek to find answers and won't give up too easily.

Girl, 12, Georgia

2

I think about
happy thoughts
and thoughts that make me cry,
I think about
angry thoughts
And though I don't know why
I think about mixed up thoughts
Of sad, of glad, of fear,
And sometimes I think about
the fact that I can think.

GIRL, 8, FLORIDA

Being gifted means having to stay in for kindergarten recess to do first-grade math.

Girl, 12, Germany

When I picture someone being gifted, I think of someone like John McEnroe or Beethoven, *not* someone in seventh grade.

Girl, 12, Arkansas

These are my feelings on being gifted:

A *A*fraid, that at some point in time I'll slip and do something wrong and everyone will notice.

G *G*uilty, when pressured into not doing my best.

I *I*solated, when others make me feel left out of, "the group."

F *F*rustrated, when I do something great and everyone laughs.

T *T*errified, when I don't know the answer and everyone stares at me.

E *E*xcited, when I create something that everyone appreciates.

D *D*isgusted, that my special needs are neglected.

P *P*rivileged, when I get extra time during school to do something for myself.

E *E*mbarrassed, when the teacher announces my grades.

R *R*elieved, when people don't laugh at me for getting less than 100%.

S *S*atisfied, when I am able to help someone else with something they don't understand.

O *O*n top of the world, when somebody says they enjoyed my work.

N *N*ervous, when pressured to always be the best.

Girl, 12, Pennyslvania

4

Speak For Yourself

1. Which response in this section comes closest to your opinion about what it means to be gifted? What would you add to it?

2. Does your school have a definition of giftedness? Find out from your teacher. If it does, ask to see a copy. How closely does it agree with the response you chose in question 1? When you compare the two, which do you like better? Why?

3. How would you answer the question, "What does it mean to be gifted?" (Be creative! Even write a poem about it, if you like.)

Are *You* Gifted?

Yes, I am gifted, and I'm not bragging, either. I think I can do my work better and that I have a high creativity level.

Girl, 10, Georgia

No, I don't think I'm smarter than other kids in my regular class. I have just been exposed to more, having had four older brothers and sisters.

Boy, 10, New York

I think I am smart because I get good grades, I do good work, I am in a gifted program, I read a lot, I study, and I think things through. I find my work is easier to do than others do. Almost everything I do I seem to do well.

Girl, 11, Arkansas

It depends on what you mean by gifted. I'm not what you would call brilliant, but I'm not dumb either. I do get some nice comments on my reading abilities, though.

Girl, 8, Illinois

I'm not gifted, just a little above average. People who are gifted are the ones that enter high school when they are thirteen.

Girl, 12, Georgia

I really don't *feel* smarter than all the other kids in my school, but I realize that I must be because I am in a program for talented children at school.

Girl, 11, Kentucky

I've never really considered myself a genius, but yes, I think I'm smart because I always seem to know the answer to the question no matter what the question might be.

Boy, 13, Georgia

I know that I'm smarter than some kids in some fields—such as theatre (when they say every word the same way) and creative writing (when every other word of theirs is something like "nice" or "big"), but I also know that in science there are many far ahead of me, and when it comes to physical education, I'm lost!

Girl, 11, New York

I think I am smart. At least that's what everyone tells me. I can read better than most kids my age and I write stories pretty well.

Boy, 12, Ontario

I don't think I'm gifted because I can always learn something from others.

Girl, 10, Connecticut

I am smart in some things, like football and dominoes, and unsmart in other subjects, like writing.

Boy, 8, Georgia

6

No, I'm not gifted. . . I just think that my brain has been trained better than most.

Boy, 12, Connecticut

I believe I was born with a special gift but I don't believe I have quite found it yet.

Boy, 13, Georgia

I really don't think I am any more gifted than any of my friends; I just work very hard at everything I do and usually I do very well.

Girl, 12, Illinois

I think I am far more intelligent than the average student. I can think, work, draw, do poetry, write stories, read, learn, express myself and speak in front of people better than the average student.

Girl, 10, British Columbia

I do think I am smarter than most kids my age, but only one way: I put my brain to use and make it do what everyone's brain *can* do if they would try to do it, or care.

Girl, 11, New York

Speak For Yourself

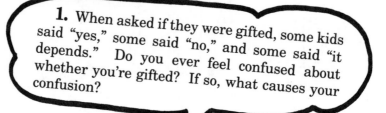

1. When asked if they were gifted, some kids said "yes," some said "no," and some said "it depends." Do you ever feel confused about whether you're gifted? If so, what causes your confusion?

2. The kids who said "yes" to the question all gave reasons why they think they're gifted. What were some of their reasons? Did you include any of these in the definition of giftedness you wrote on page 5.

3. Think of some of the people who know you. Now think of at least two who would probably call you gifted. What would their reasons be? Now think of at least two who would probably *not* call you gifted. What would their reasons be?

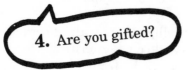

4. Are you gifted?

How Did You Find Out You Were Gifted?

When I was first born. My doctor told my mother and my mother told me.

Girl, 13, Georgia

When I was two. My mom told me that I read Donald Duck books to my brother, who was one.

Girl, 12, Mississippi

My family learned that I was gifted when I was two years old and my mother's friend gave me a grade 8 puzzle and I finished it in twenty minutes.

Boy, 11, Connecticut

I found out in nursery school when I was the only one who could read.

Girl, 7, Arkansas

I found out I was gifted in nursery school when I was told I was skipping kindergarten.

Boy, 10, Connecticut

I discovered being gifted on my own, more or less, because I taught myself how to read when I was in kindergarten, and from then on I always seemed to do better than everyone (except in athletics).

Boy, 13, Georgia

When I was in first grade I had a series of tests that other children didn't take. My scores were sent home one day and my mother showed me my IQ and told me my scores and that I would be in a special class because I was smart.

Boy, 11, Georgia

In second grade; it was announced over the intercom.

Girl, 12, Georgia

In first grade in a first/second mixed class. I would use big words and even the second graders didn't know what I meant.

Girl, 10, Maryland

I would read my brother's school papers when he brought them home.

Girl, 11, Nebraska

I learned I was gifted when second grade was easy.

Boy, 9, Texas

In third grade. I was in school on a Tuesday afternoon and my teacher called me into the hall and broke it to me easy.

Boy, 11, Georgia

I learned I was gifted on September 12, 1982. I found out when I got a letter from my teacher.

Boy, 10, British Columbia

I learned I was gifted from my mother. (Intelligence is hereditary in our family.)

Girl, 10, Louisiana

I found out in third grade. I always finished my work early and would disturb others because I had nothing to do.

Girl, 12, North Carolina

In grade four, although I had the suspicion since grade two.

Boy, 10, British Columbia

When I passed the gifted test my mommy told me.

Girl, 7, Louisiana

My parents recognized me as being gifted very early, but I wasn't tested until fourth grade.

Boy, 12, Arkansas

I learned I was gifted in fourth grade when our program for gifted children started. All kids who showed extra intelligence were recommended for it by teachers and parents.

Girl, 12, Arkansas

I've been in a gifted program since fourth grade but I didn't know I was "gifted" until sixth grade when we were given these pamphlets on what being gifted really meant.

Girl, 13, Georgia

Speak For Yourself

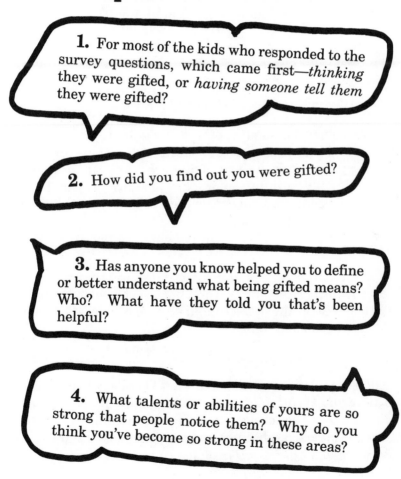

1. For most of the kids who responded to the survey questions, which came first—*thinking* they were gifted, or *having someone tell them* they were gifted?

2. How did you find out you were gifted?

3. Has anyone you know helped you to define or better understand what being gifted means? Who? What have they told you that's been helpful?

4. What talents or abilities of yours are so strong that people notice them? Why do you think you've become so strong in these areas?

How Are You the Same As Other Kids Your Age? How Are You Different?

I'm the same because I'm just a regular kid and I'm different because in most cases, when a teacher calls on me I can answer right away, where most kids have to think a second.

Girl, 13, Georgia

I used to think (and sometimes still do think) that my ideas are weird. My friends don't have ideas, well, as deep as mine.

Girl, 11, Louisiana

I'm just different because I'm a little smarter, but that's not to say I'm really any *better* than anyone else.

Boy, 9, Georgia

I think about the same as others in my class except I *want* to learn and they just want to rush through so they can have fun. I'm different from them in many ways. I can pick up a book and really get interested. They just pick it up and put it down. I also think I am *determined* to do certain things— they just do it if they can.

Girl, 11, North Carolina

I still make mistakes and sometimes get bad grades. I know a little more about the world because I lived in Europe, and I am a little ahead of them in science because I'm from a different school system.

Girl, 11, Georgia

I don't really do much different, but I challenge my teachers more and argue points and insights more than the other kids (who take the teacher's word for everything). I love to argue with teachers, but not just for the sake of arguing.

Girl, 13, Ohio

I like to talk and laugh just like other kids. I'm different because sometimes I think the "in crowd" is a little bit silly.

Girl, 11, Arkansas

I ask the same questions, but on a more intellectual basis. I have a larger vocabulary, though, and a different sense of humor.

Boy, 13, Georgia

I enjoy playing the same games as my classmates, but I also enjoy doing harder work than my friends. Also, I'm different because I love homework.

Girl, 7, Louisiana

I am the same as other children in my classroom because we are all funny and smart. I'm different because some others are kinder than me.

Boy, 9, Connecticut

I can assimilate information well. I usually only need things explained once. But I make mistakes like everyone else and I ask questions when I don't understand.

Girl, 10, Georgia

I enjoy quiet rather than screaming, but sometimes I still jump on my bike and burn off in the hills to get dirty. That's another thing the same about kids—dirt.

Girl, 10, British Columbia

I love to read and I could read all day long. Kids think I am weird because I read so much. But if that makes me different, I plan on staying that way.

Girl, 10, Kentucky

I'm the same because I get into trouble for talking and I like to go to lunch and visit. I'm different because I don't like recess—I'd rather be working on a project.

Boy, 9, Arkansas

I am the same as other kids in that we know a lot of things and we can think logically, but the difference lies in how we interpret things and how creative we are. Another difference is how we show our knowledge of things, beyond just knowing the answer.

Boy, 10, Ohio

I really don't feel I'm different from anyone else. I might be a little chubby but I don't feel like I'm any different.

Girl, 11, Arkansas

I feel that I relate to adults relatively better than others my own age. I also feel that I have more ambition than most people my age. On the outside, though, I'm pretty much the same—I enjoy going places with friends and having a good time. But if I don't have my homework done, I can't enjoy myself, while most people my age don't let that bother them.

Girl, 13, Georgia

Speak For Yourself

1. How are you the same as other kids your age? How are you different? Do you think of your differences as positive or negative? Why?

2. Think about your best friend. In what ways are you the same? In what ways are you different? Now think about someone you don't like at all. In what ways are you the same? In what ways are you different?

3. Do you think being gifted means you're a "better person"? (Discuss this question with a teacher or friend if possible.)

14

How Do You Feel about the Word "Gifted"?

 **I Like It!**

I really do not mind being called gifted. It is not an absurd name like some people think, and it doesn't embarrass me. It is sort of like a praise when you're called gifted.

Girl, 11, Georgia

I don't mind being called gifted as long as I'm not stereotyped as being perfect.

Boy, 9, Georgia

I like being called gifted but only if it doesn't interfere with my friends. For example, I'm sure most people would be annoyed if their friend was constantly called "gifted" while no one said a thing to them.

Girl, 11, Indiana

I think the word gifted is perfect, because it means we have a "gift" to understand things others don't.

Girl, 13, Georgia

I like being called gifted because it makes me feel special, but when I think about it I don't want to be gifted because I want to be the same as my friends.

Boy, 11, Connecticut

I'd rather be called gifted than smarty pants!

Boy, 12, Georgia

I Don't Like It!

I do not like being called gifted; it's embarrassing and it's like bragging.

Boy, 9, New Mexico

15

I don't like being called gifted because it makes me feel like an object and not my own individual person. I don't think we should be "called" anything. We were just born smarter than others and can't help it. When people call me a "gifted child" it makes me angry.

Girl, 12, Georgia

I really feel uncomfortable with the word gifted. It makes me feel like I am covered with wrapping paper and tied up in a bow.

Girl, 12, Connecticut

Being called gifted is fine, but when a teacher brings it up I feel like an outsider, considering most of my friends aren't gifted. One child in class who has an IQ of about one million (exaggeration) often talks to "not gifted" kids like "I'm gifted and you're not, so ha! ha!" So, in other words, it's OK for teacher-talk and recommendations for things, but around my class "gifted" is almost a kind of mean, discriminating word.

Boy, 11, Connecticut

I don't like being called gifted because people expect too much of me.

Girl, 10, Louisiana

I am constantly being reminded how smart I am and it's getting pretty sickening.

Girl, 11, Illinois

I Think They Should Use Another Word

When I think of a gifted person, I think of an eerie old man with a long beard, little spectacles, and lots of wrinkles. A name I would like better would be "over-average student." I like this name better because it doesn't make me sound like a genius.

Boy, 11, Ohio

"Gifted" sounds too powerful. I think the term "capable children" is better because it doesn't sound as if you have E.S.P.

> Girl, 11, British Columbia

I like the word "special" better than "gifted" because it does not necessarily refer to being very smart.

> Girl, 11, Louisiana

I would rather be called a "better thinker".

> Boy, 10, British Columbia

Being called gifted isn't something you like or dislike, it's really something you cope with whether you like it or not. I would rather be called "talented" or "well above average."

> Girl, 10, North Carolina

Forget "gifted," and use "intelligent"; it's more subtle.

> Boy, 11, Arkansas

I don't know of any other word to replace "gifted" but I wish someone would think of something.

> Girl, 12, Georgia

Speak For Yourself

1. Which response do you agree with the most? Which do you agree with the least? Explain your answers.

2. How do you feel about the word "gifted"?

3. Do you think people should use another word besides "gifted" to describe persons with high abilities? Can you think of a better word? What makes your word better?

17

Do You Think Special Programs for the Gifted Are a Good Idea?

 **Yes!**

Gifted programs give kids a chance to stay smart.

Boy, 11, Georgia

I think gifted classes are a good idea because kids get bored in school and might start getting bad grades.

Boy, 9, New York

I think that all schools should have gifted programs because they give gifted children a chance to *really* use their brain.

Boy, 9, Ohio

If you're in a class that's easy, you're not learning anything.

Boy, 11, New York

I like to be around children who are as intelligent as I am.

Boy, 11, North Carolina

People who *can* do harder work or *can* go to special classes should be able to *get* what they deserve.

Girl, 12, New York

Some people don't like their classmates or teachers and need to get away for part of the day. They already know most of the work in their classrooms so they need a special program.

Boy, 12, New York

Without the gifted program I would have no reason to go to school.

Girl, 12, New York

I believe that special programs are important because without them I wouldn't be able to learn anything extra and I wouldn't have any competition.

Boy, 12, California

I believe you should have a special class for special kids so that they can learn faster. Because when a child is kept from learning, he or she will become frustrated.

Girl, 12, Michigan

Schools should have gifted programs, but also they should have other special programs (such as art, physical education, music, etc.) for the rest of the kids who have other special talents.

Girl, 12, Illinois

 **No!**

No. Gifted programs make you miss your other classes and they make other kids jealous, too.

Girl, 9, Illinois

I think that maybe gifted students should have a special program but it should not take up regular classroom time. Sure, the students might be getting out of class, but we miss important lessons and we have to stay in for recess to learn them.

Girl, 11, Connecticut

Why not have anyone who is interested in something and has a special ability get time to work on it?

Girl, 11, New York

I think that you should not have a program for children that are skilled because I think it affects the whole class and makes them feel bad. I think we could have our meetings in the classroom just as well.

Girl, 8, Illinois

Speak For Yourself

1. Look back at the responses to this question. Using these responses, make a list of the "pros" (the good points) of gifted programs and another list of the "cons" (the bad points) of gifted programs. Now add your own opinions to both lists.

2. Imagine that you're a member of the school board. The board is voting on whether to start a gifted program in your school. Half of the members have voted "yes" and the other half have voted "no. " *You* get to cast the final vote. What will you decide? (How could you try to convince others that your opinion is the best one?)

3. How do you think schools should decide who does and doesn't get into a gifted program? List the things you believe they should consider (for example: IQ, grades, classroom behavior, teacher recommendations, kids' own opinions). What requirements that aren't academic (for example: leadership abilities, athletic abilities, talent in art or music) might you consider?

4. Now find out how your school decides who does and doesn't get into a gifted program. Ask your teacher for a copy of the guidelines your school uses. How do they compare with the ones you listed in Question 3? Which do you think are better?

5. Do you think special programs for the gifted are a good idea? Why or why not?

How Do You Feel about the Program You're In?

At first I was scared, but now I really like it.

Girl, 8, Louisiana

Before gifted classes came along I was bored of the same old stuff six and a half hours a day, five days a week. I don't know where I'd be without my gifted classes.

Boy, 9, California

I love my gifted program. It sort of makes me want to give an extra effort. Being in our gifted program makes me feel proud of myself.

Girl, 11, Georgia

In a regular class there is only one right answer to questions, but here there are lots of correct answers.

Girl, 11, British Columbia

I love it! I have to make up work, and sometimes I have to stay in for recess to get it done, but my gifted program is the brightest part of my day.

Boy, 11, North Carolina

It gives me an hour out of every day to do the things I really enjoy and to just be "me."

Girl, 13, Georgia

In a regular class a gifted person gets bored silly. We need someone to push us beyond mediocrity.

Boy, 12, Georgia

I don't like it anymore. I've been in my gifted program since third grade and now I'm in seventh; we always do the same thing and most of the girls and a few of the boys are snobs.

Boy, 12, Georgia

I like being in a gifted program. It's nice to work with other kids who don't have to look at my papers for the right answer.

Girl, 7, Wyoming

The kids are great and you feel like you've known them all your life. The teachers are the best and can help you with anything from acrophobia to zoos. I should know—I've been here since fourth grade and have never missed a day!

Boy, 11, Connecticut

Being in a gifted program gives me a chance to say what I feel about something and not be laughed at. I *like* to be understood.

Girl, 11, Georgia

I like being in gifted because it is fun to do extra work, plus we are a small group so it is easy to concentrate.

Boy, 10, Georgia

It's neat; you're treated more like adults.

Boy, 13, Mississippi

Without extras like the gifted program, school turns into a monotonous circle of turn-in-your-papers, listen, ignore and be ignored.

Girl, 12, Kentucky

I've enjoyed being in all the gifted programs I've participated in because they are always small classes. The smaller the class, the more of a friendship you can build with others. I was able to relate better to my last year's teacher (gifted teacher) than almost anyone I've ever known (except, of course, my twin brother).

Boy, 12, North Carolina

We have 99.7% more freedom.

Boy, 10, Arizona

Being in a gifted program
May not be like you think.
Some kids think you're great
and some kids think you stink.
It's not free time; it is work,
But whatever you choose to do,
It's a nice, polite environment
With teachers to help you.
Your peer group may pressure you,
So choose who you want to be.
Just remember: everyone is unique—
You are you and I am me.

BOY, 11, CONNECTICUT

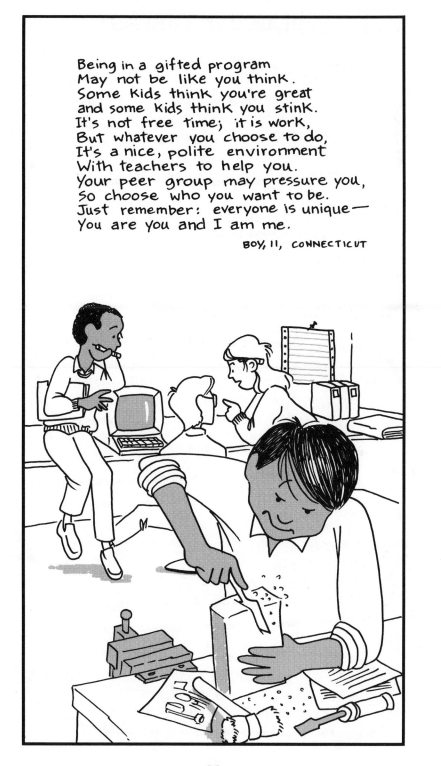

Speak For Yourself

1. What did you expect from your gifted program *before* you started it? What did you think would happen in it? What did you think you would get out of it?

2. Now that you're in the program, is it better or worse than you expected? Give some reasons for your opinion.

3. How do you feel about the program you're in? Would you recommend it to a friend who was trying to decide whether or not to be in the gifted and talented (g/t) program?

4. What things about your g/t program would you change? What would you leave the same? Write down some of your ideas. Then talk them over with your parents. Maybe you and your parents can talk to the person in charge of your gifted program—and maybe some of your ideas can be put into action!

5. Can you predict a time when you will no longer need to be in a gifted program? What would you do instead to challenge yourself?

CHAPTER 2

◆◆◆◆◆◆◆◆◆◆◆◆◆◆◆◆◆◆◆◆◆◆◆◆◆◆

Getting Along With Friends And Other Kids At School

◆◆◆◆◆◆◆◆◆◆◆◆◆◆◆◆◆◆◆◆◆◆◆◆◆◆

How Do People Treat You When They Know You're Gifted?

My good friends are happy that I have special abilities.

Girl, 9, California

One of my unfriends makes fun of me.

Girl, 8, Kansas

My friends treat me good. They say, "That's a good story, Bobby" and "You're doing good in school." They don't make me feel bad.

Boy, 6, Illinois

My friends don't really mind me being gifted, or at least they haven't shown they mind. They really never say anything—good or bad.

Boy, 12, Georgia

They treat me as if I wasn't there, they play tricks on me, and they exclude me from their games.

Girl, 10, Kentucky

25

I am considerably lucky to have friends that understand it's a very precious gift to be talented in many ways. Some friends of mine compliment my work, which is nice. Others say cruel things (which I don't care to mention).

Girl, 13, Connecticut

Most of my friends act very nice to me, not because of my abilities but because of who I am.

Girl, 10, Pennsylvania

Last year, G.T. stood for *G*arbage and *T*rash or *G*ifted *T*urkeys. This year, when we got back from our gifted (g/t) program some kids go "YUCK! G.T.s." It makes me feel like smacking them, but usually I don't.

Girl, 10, Louisiana

My friends treat me the same as their other friends, but sometimes they compliment me and that makes me feel good.

Girl, 10, Ohio

On the days I have my gifted program, Martha isn't my friend. Other days she likes me.

Girl, 8, Pennsylvania

My friends react to my abilities by calling me "school boy." They call me other names like that too. It used to bother me but now it doesn't.

Boy, 9, California

The kids in my class call me "bookworm" just because I read a lot more than most of the kids in my class.

Boy, 9, Wyoming

My friends don't say anything about me being different and I'm glad. When they ask me for help it makes me feel good that I can help them. I never feel bad about being gifted but sometimes I wish some other kids were more interested in some of the things I am.

Girl, 9, Connecticut

My friends treat me like any other of their friends. I like it that way.

Girl, 8, Ohio

They try to get me to do their work for them.

Girl, 11, Puerto Rico

The don't even notice.

Girl, 7, Maine

Kids I don't know tease me. Our teacher calls us "Champs" and the other kids call us "Chumps."

Girl, 11, California

Some of my friends treat me like an encyclopedia, which makes me wonder if they are friends or users.

Boy, 11, Illinois

I am very lucky because I have really great friends. My friends accept me for what I am and they don't mind when I go to a different school for my gifted program. They don't mind when I talk to them about such topics as science and government, instead of baseball and football.

Boy, 12, Virginia

My friends really aren't jealous because a lot of them go to special classes and so they know if they tease me they'll get the same thing in return.

Girl, 10, Maine

One friend says that I act cool because I am in a third-grade room for reading and math, but none of my other friends say anything. I don't feel I act cool.

Girl, 7, Illinois

My friends ask me for help when they don't understand something. They don't tease or make fun of me but appreciate my help.

Boy, 12, Virginia

27

PROFESSOR

"Professor"'s what they call me
I'm Known throughout the school
As some straight-laced goody-goody
Who never breaks a rule.
If I get in trouble
It makes the news headlines—
I guess it's a conspiracy
To be among good minds.

I wish they Knew
the real me,
the one that stays
inside,
the one Known to my
"gifted" friends
But, to others, stays
inside.

GIRL, 13, OHIO

I've gotten almost all my spelling tests, reading tests, and math tests right. Some of the other kids don't at all. So, they either say "You cheated" or "The teacher spends more time with you." I really hate it. It drives me crazy.

Girl, 9, New Jersey

Sometimes one boy always sticks out his tongue and makes a face when I get a better grade than he does.

Girl, 11, Ohio

There is one girl in my class who has no respect for anyone else's feelings. She makes fun of me for being gifted. Sometimes I wish I could be dumb. Other people just expect me to do well and when I don't, they make fun of me. I wish I could be like everybody and be accepted by everyone.

Girl, 11, Massachusetts

When we talk about report cards, my friends sometimes say I was "teacher's pet" and that's why I got straight A's. It bugs me to know my friends feel that way about me.

Girl, 10, California

Most of the kids seem to like me but sometimes I think it's because they can copy my answers. Some of them like me for myself but others treat me like some form of cast-off.

Boy, 11, Ohio

Some get jealous, others call me a "brain," but my real friends don't do either of these things—I respect them for that.

Girl, 12, Illinois

I am more active in more intellectual types of groups and clubs, and for that I am sneered at, called names, and looked down at. But I try not to let it get me down because I know the other kids are just jealous, but somehow this makes it difficult to participate in other activities at school (example: I am always the last one picked for a softball team in P.E.).

Girl, 13, Georgia

My peer group is mostly made up of gifted students. Those that aren't don't think of us as any different. Actually, I've never stopped to think about how I'm smarter than they are. I like to think of myself as just an average person, although grown-ups always tell me not to think that way.

Girl, 11, Illinois

If you are gifted, don't pay attention to what children say about it—just remember, if you work to the best of your ability, and *you* know *yourself* that you are doing what's right (which I must remind myself of often when I'm under peer pressure), that's all that counts.

Girl, 13, Georgia

Speak For Yourself

1. Give an example of how people treat you when they know you're gifted.

2. How do you act when someone compliments you on being gifted? Has anyone ever "put you down" for being gifted? How did it feel? How did you react?

3. Think of some "positive comebacks" to compliments. (Examples: "Thank you," "It's nice to know you like my work," "I feel good when you say things like that.") Now think of some "positive comebacks" to not-so-nice words and actions. (Examples: "It makes me feel bad when you call me a brain," "I wish you wouldn't stick out your tongue at me when I get a good grade on a test.") Write down some of your ideas. Talk them over with your parents and teachers. Practice saying them aloud so you're prepared the next time you need a "positive comeback."

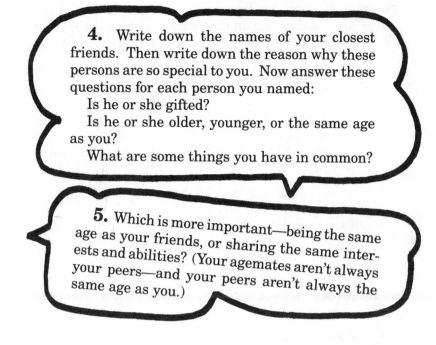

4. Write down the names of your closest friends. Then write down the reason why these persons are so special to you. Now answer these questions for each person you named:

Is he or she gifted?

Is he or she older, younger, or the same age as you?

What are some things you have in common?

5. Which is more important—being the same age as your friends, or sharing the same interests and abilities? (Your agemates aren't always your peers—and your peers aren't always the same age as you.)

Do You Ever Try to Hide the Fact That You're Gifted?

I try to hide my abilities so my friend Herman won't think I'm a show-off. And I don't like not being liked. And I am not a show-off.

Boy, 9, Alaska

Sometimes we'll do an easy thing and I'll take my time to look like I'm just as puzzled as everyone else.

Girl, 9, Illinois

Yes. . . from my best friend. She is not too smart and I'm afraid I'll lose my best friend if I'm smart.

Girl, 9, Kentucky

I think it is special to be gifted and I never hide it.

Boy, 7, Michigan

Sometimes when my friends talk about "how hard the test was" or "I did so bad on that test" and I did well, I just don't say anything that might hurt their feelings or offend them.

Girl, 11, Michigan

There are times I try to act "dumb." The reason I do this is because some of my friends aren't very bright—they feel uncomfortable when I act gifted, so I act dumb to make them feel comfortable.

Boy, 12, Kentucky

No. . . if you've got it why not use it? What is the problem with being smart?

Boy, 10, New York

The only time I try to hide the fact that I am gifted is when I am with friends or other kids and want to "fit in" or be a part of a group.

Boy, 12, Connecticut

No. I'm proud of the fact that I'm gifted. Since I'm not popular or pretty, I feel that I have to have something to make myself accepted, so I rely on my gifted ability.

Girl, 12, Kentucky

I never try to hide being gifted because there is no reason to be ashamed of it.

Boy, 12, New York

I don't think that I should ever hide what I am. You should never hide what you are because then people will never know what you are inside. I have come to the point in my life where my friends like me for what I am. When I was in fourth grade the only reason I had friends was so they could copy off my tests.

Girl, 13, New Jersey

Speak For Yourself

1. Do you ever try to hide the fact that you're gifted?

2. Think of a time when you hid your giftedness or felt like hiding it. Why did you want to do this?

3. Do you think it's a good idea to hide your abilities? What might happen to a gifted kid who did this a lot?

4. Some kids who responded to this question seemed very comfortable with letting their giftedness show. Do you think it's easier for some kids? Why might this be so? How is it for you— easy or hard? What do you think you could do to make it easier?

5. The next time you feel like hiding your giftedness, what could you do instead?

How Do You Feel about Being Smarter Than Some of Your Friends?

Well, sometimes someone asks me a question and I'm glad to answer it, but sometimes I'm sorry they don't know the answer themselves.

Girl, 8, Illinois

My friend Kris keeps bugging me about going to my gifted program. He says, "I'd sure like to go to QUEST." It makes me feel good, because he'd like to go. It makes me feel bad because he keeps bugging me about it.

Boy, 8, Maine

Whenever I'm doing my work and I get something right while others get it wrong, they say, "Sally's so much more smarter than us." That makes me feel good and bad at different times. It makes me feel *good* when they laugh after they say it but it makes me feel *bad* when they make a face.

Girl, 11, Pennsylvania

If someone is talking about a topic and I tell them what I know about it, they seem to think that I am bragging. . . and I don't mean for it to be that way! I just try to share my knowledge with them but they take it that I am bragging. Now I'm careful of who I say things in front of.

Boy, 11, Connecticut

Cold shoulders, dirty looks, and smirks hurt a lot more than somebody coming right out and saying something horrible.

Girl, 11, Michigan

Sometimes when I get better marks on a test than others, I ask my friend what she got. Then I tell her my mark and she says, "Why should I tell you; now that you're in that gifted class all you do is brag." I don't get very mad at this— hurt, yes, but not mad. I am starting to understand why she does it, but sometimes I feel I am all alone.

Girl, 11, British Columbia

If my friends ask me a question and I find I don't know the answer, they sometimes complain and say, "I thought you were supposed to be smart." It depends on my feelings whether I get mad or not, but usually I don't get too upset.

Girl, 11, Connecticut

Speak For Yourself

1. Some people think that gifted kids are bragging when they aren't, or that they're trying to "show off" when they're just being themselves. Can you remember a time when people have thought or said these things about you or someone you know?

2. How do you feel about being smarter than some of your friends?

3. Have you ever refused to tell other kids your grades even when they asked? If so, why? When you talk to kids who aren't in the gifted program, do you act any differently than when you talk to kids who are in the program? If so, why?

4. Can you remember a time when you let your abilities show and felt proud of yourself? What did other people say and do?

5. Can you remember a time when you helped someone else feel proud of his or her abilities? What did you say and do?

6. Write a classified ad that starts with the words, "WANTED: One friend. Must be. . ." Now complete it by listing the qualities and characteristics you think are important in a friend.

35

CHAPTER 3

◆◆◆◆◆◆◆◆◆◆◆◆◆◆◆◆◆◆◆◆◆◆◆◆◆◆◆

Handling Expectations (Yours And Everyone Else's)

◆◆◆◆◆◆◆◆◆◆◆◆◆◆◆◆◆◆◆◆◆◆◆◆◆◆◆

What Do You Expect from Yourself?

Sometimes I'm really smart, but when it matters and I goof, it breaks my heart.

> Girl, 10, New York

I expect a lot of good work from myself.

> Girl, 10, Illinois

Sometime I feel like "Oh, no! What if I get a bad grade! Mom'll just kill me!" But I *know* I won't make a grade that bad, because it never has happened and it never will.

> Girl, 10, Louisiana

I sometimes feel I need to do something all my own way, something only mine, that I can be proud of.

It might seem reasonable that it would be easy for a gifted child to get too self-conscious and expect to always get good grades. For me, it's always fear that I'll do horribly, and fearing a tirade from a teacher.

> Boy, 11, Michigan

37

I love A's, and the first time I got a B, I cried. But I only got one. No more of those B's.

Girl, 11, Connecticut

I'm disappointed when I fail to accomplish something but I try to accept it and try again and again until I get it right. I'm proud of high achievements...but still, I yearn for higher ones.

Boy, 12, Michigan

I know if I had a test with anyone my age I would probably win hands down. People say I have too much self-confidence—but I think I have just enough.

Girl, 11, Massachusetts

I think I push myself harder than my parents do. They have always accepted my getting good grades and when I get a bad grade I think I am more disappointed than my parents. When I set goals for myself they are quite high, and when I don't reach them I become downfallen, and sometimes I feel like there is no point in life and that I want to run away and who cares about school anyway. But I always get at it again and try even harder.

Girl, 11, Michigan

Sometimes I wish I didn't get all A's. First, because everyone makes fun of me and second, because it shows that I'm not really being challenged. I don't do as much as I could, but I get straight A's anyway.

Girl, 12, Pennsylvania

I sort of like getting the highest mark because I really feel good after I've accomplished that. I feel like everything's off my back, like all that pressure.

Girl, 10, Connecticut

I think I am harder on myself than anyone else. For instance, if I get a B on something then I will be very disappointed. I don't think that I push myself too hard—I just get upset if I don't do well.

Boy, 11, Michigan

I am a reasonably lazy person, so I do usually just what I can get by with.

Girl, 10, Georgia

Now that I'm in a gifted program, I push myself harder. I get mad at myself if I don't get good grades, and I wonder what will happen next.

Boy, 12, Michigan

39

Sometimes I feel pressured into being always better than average. Every once in a while I just want to be below average.

Girl, 12, Kansas

I am waiting for the day I can face a blank page without fear, for the day I will stop running away from discovering myself and turn around to see what life's all about.

Girl, 12, Pennsylvania

I feel that I should work for a grade and then get what I deserve. I like to get A's and B's on my report card and personally won't accept anything below that.

Girl, 11, Connecticut

The competition definitely gets harder when you get into higher grades, since everyone wants to be number one. I realize it's nice to win when you compete against others, but the most important part is beating yourself!

Boy, 12, Michigan

Speak For Yourself

1. Have you ever envied other kids because they were more popular than you are, or better at sports, or better in some other way? Why do you think you envied these people?

2. Imagine that you're creating a commercial about yourself. The purpose is to try to "sell" yourself to someone who doesn't know you. What would you do and say? Which of your strengths and abilities would you bring out in your commercial?

3. How do you feel when you get A's? Do you think that good grades are a true reflection of your abilities? (In other words, have you ever gotten an A without having had to think much or do much work?)

4. What makes an A worth getting? Is a high grade in a hard subject more meaningful than a high grade in an easy subject? Think back to some of the A's you've gotten. Which ones have meant the most to you? Why?

5. Do you think that schools should use other ways besides grades to measure progress and achievement? List some of those ways. Talk them over with your parents and teachers.

What Do Others Expect from You?

Some people expect me to talk with big words, act right all the time, not be athletic, do things like staying inside all day reading. I do read, but not every second of my life.

Boy, 11, Connecticut

Some children at school expect me to be conceited or to brag about myself. I don't do this, though. For one thing, it makes the person who's bragging look like a fool, and secondly, I don't have to brag to feel proud of myself.

Girl, 11, California

My friends expect me to be a "goody two-shoes" because I'm in the gifted program, and they expect me to get straight A+'s. If I get an A instead, they say, "You should do better."

Girl, 11, Connecticut

My mom thinks I should be able to hear better.

> Girl, 8, Maine

When report cards come out everybody wants to know what I got. They expect me to have the best grades in the school.

> Boy, 11, Connecticut

My friends think I should know everything. I hate that! They should treat me like everybody else.

> Girl, 10, Connecticut

At home my brother thinks I'm so smart that I am able to do all of his homework.

> Girl, 10, Kansas

Lots of friends say, "If you're so smart, I bet you can't do this." I really hate that. When people want me to do something that takes muscles, which has nothing to do with mental content, I get even angrier. It makes me mad!

> Boy, 10, Georgia

My teacher expects me to act differently. She expects me to check out harder books, to have better answers, and to do more.

> Boy, 8, Colorado

At home, when I get in a fight with my brother, my parents will say, "June, you're an intelligent girl, but you sure don't have much common sense." At school, teachers say, "You should be a pleasure to work with, but you're sure not acting gifted today. I should be able to give you an assignment and you should have it done the next day."

> Girl, 12, California

If I fail a test (which is likely for an average seventh grader) I am looked at as if I should be hanged because that is not expected of a child of "my ability."

> Boy, 11, Connecticut

In school, our P.E. teacher criticizes things our class does differently and says we are "gifted children who should be setting an example," as if a gifted child is perfect. *She* thinks we should be perfect.

Girl, 11, Virginia

Adults think I should act like a grown-up, not be any fun, and not play with anybody who's not in the gifted program.

Boy, 10, Illinois

At home, no one expects me to act differently; they just expect me to act like any other kid. At school, they expect me to get better grades, speak better, and have better manners.

Boy, 10, Connecticut

Sometimes when I act silly my mom says, "Don't do that" or "Don't say that; you're too smart to do that." Sometimes, too, she says, "Get harder and bigger books from the library." And I do (or don't).

Girl, 9, Ohio

People usually expect me to be a "perfect example" and angel, or just plain ol' brilliant. If I bring home a math paper (or whatever) and I got a C or D on it, my Mom will say, "Ellen! I'm surprised at you!" because she expects me to be the smart one of the family (and because I'm a teacher's daughter).

Girl, 11, Illinois

Teachers expect me to be very organized, and I definitely am not!

Girl, 10, Illinois

Because I have previously shown I am capable of getting good grades and understanding schoolwork, of course I am expected to "keep it up." Because of this, maybe, my teachers and parents expect me to grasp things more quickly and they have less patience with me if I don't. (But this often proves to be no great problem.)

Girl, 12, Wyoming

If I ever misbehave at home my parents will say, "And to think you are in a gifted program!" It can really start to bug me.

Girl, 12, Illinois

One of my teachers expects me to explain answers. The others expect me to be able to answer questions the other kids can't answer.

Girl, 9, Illinois

Some of my teachers say I should get all A's and if I slack off they get very mad. They'll take me out in the hall and talk to me about it. I try to walk away, but instead, I usually stand there and don't listen. I may be smart, I may slack off, but I never got a C in my life.

Boy, 11, Connecticut

My parents are gently but surely pushing me, while my teachers literally make me do more work. This is a depressing subject. Let's get off it.

Girl, 11, Illinois

Speak For Yourself

1. Complete each of these sentences:

- When I get an A in school...
- Most of my friends expect me to...
- When report cards come out...
- I do best in school when...
- I like school when...
- I like my friends best when...
- Some of my teachers expect me to...
- If I fail a test...
- When I get a compliment about my work...
- My parents expect me to...
- No one expects me to...

44

2. How do the things you expect from yourself compare with the things other people expect from you? Are they the same, a little bit different, or very different? If they're very different, what could you do to bring them closer together?

3. Do you think that people have a right to expect things from you? When are someone else's expectations okay—and when aren't they?

4. Do you have a right to expect things from other people? What kinds of things?

What Happens When You Make a Mistake?

When I make mistakes, my parents and uncle just tell me to start over, and my friends never say anything. But sometimes grownups say something really dumb like "Oh, Einstein, I thought you could do everything."

Boy, 6, Vermont

When I make a mistake, I usually fell like disappearing because I know the kids in my class and my teachers expect more.

Boy, 9, Wyoming

Emily laughs. Beth doesn't do anything. I just correct it.

Girl, 9, Kansas

I think most people like to see me make mistakes because they get tired of me always getting good grades. They want to prove to themselves that I can't do everything perfect.

Girl, 12, Illinois

I feel embarrassed. Sometimes I feel so embarrassed I cry.

Girl, 8, Ohio

I just say to myself, "I'll just try harder next time." I don't think it's such a big deal when I do something wrong.

Girl, 10, California

Here, people tease and taunt you if you make a mistake. I've had it happen to me before. People here support only those people with more muscle and less brain.

Boy, 11, California

Some kids at school think I have to be right all of the time. If I'm not, then there's something wrong, they think. That doesn't bother me, though; I just let it go by most of the time.

Girl, 13, South Dakota

I get very sad and mad and sometimes I want to rumple my papers so nobody has to see them! At the beginning of first grade (now I'm in second) I didn't even want to do creative writing because I was afraid I wouldn't write exactly what the teacher wanted and she would say I made a mistake.

Girl, 7, New York

When nobody knows I've made a mistake I try to cover it up and make it look as if it *were* supposed to happen.

Boy, 12, Virginia

People act the same as if someone else makes a mistake. But because I seldom get in trouble, if I do, my teachers always tell me how embarrassed I should be.

Boy, 11, Georgia

People are frequently *offended* when I make a mistake, or they pounce on me for making it. In return, I am inclined to be cynical, sarcastic, and embarrassed towards them.

Girl, 13, Wyoming

When I make a mistake everybody acts like I suddenly lost my brain. I feel very uncomfortable with this feeling.

Boy, 10, Georgia

When I make a mistake others laugh, and so do I.

Girl, 10, Texas

When I make a mistake, some people are nice and help me find the answer. That makes me feel better about my mistakes. Some kids laugh and make fun of me. That makes me so angry that I want to punch them in the nose. But I don't do that because it isn't nice.

Girl, 7, New York

I throw away my paper.

Boy, 10, Connecticut

People compare how many mistakes I make and how many they make, and if I have more it just gives them a mental pat on the back. If I have fewer, they just think it's normal.

Girl, 11, Connecticut

I don't go by mistakes that I make but rather the ones I solve or correct.

Girl, 11, Connecticut

I try to hide all of my mistakes so I don't get teased.

Girl, 10, Connecticut

I turn red.

Boy, 13, Connecticut

Speak For Yourself

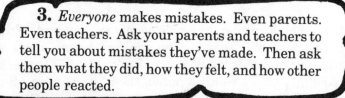

1. What happens when you make a mistake? (What do you do? How do you feel? How do other people react?)

2. Do you ever feel pressured to be perfect? If so, give an example of when you feel pressured. Tell how you feel when it happens.

3. *Everyone* makes mistakes. Even parents. Even teachers. Ask your parents and teachers to tell you about mistakes they've made. Then ask them what they did, how they felt, and how other people reacted.

4. Has anyone ever told you, "It's okay to make a mistake. We all learn through our mistakes." Can you think of a time when some-one said this to you? What was your mistake, and what did you learn from it?

Do You Ever Just
"Go along with the Crowd"?

Yes, but most of the time I do what my conscience tells me to do.

Girl, 9, Ohio

Sometimes I do go along just to fit in with the crowd. For instance, when my friends are playing something I'm really not interested in and I want to play with them, I play it.

Girl, 10, California

Very rarely! If my friends are playing a really stupid game, a lot of times I'll just tell them that the game doesn't excite me.

Girl, 10, New York

Yes... because when I feel left out I feel like nobody likes me anymore.

Boy, 11, California

I usually don't do anything to fit in with the crowd. There are my friends and other people who like me just the way I am so I don't try to be someone I'm not. My mom and dad taught me the difference between right and wrong, so I know how to make good judgments.

Girl, 11, California

Because I am gifted I can see that a lot of the things my peers do will appear silly or foolish to other people, and that some of the things they do could be potentially dangerous. Mostly, I try to stay out of those kinds of situations. However, in such a large junior high, I inevitably find myself in situations I don't like. When I don't go along with the group, people (my peers) often ridicule me or insult me, which hurts a lot, but I try not to let it bug me. In general, I would say I go along with the crowd except when I think it will hurt myself or others, physically or mentally.

Girl, 13, Wyoming

I do things to go along with the crowd—like asking questions I know the answers to just so they will treat me like one of them.

Boy, 11, Illinois

Very often I persuade people to do what I want; usually I am a leader.

Boy, 9, California

I do a lot of things to go along with the crowd, and when I decide to do things for myself, I very rarely come out ahead.

Boy, 10, Texas

If I decided I didn't want to do what my friends wanted me to do, I wouldn't have any friends.

Girl, 12, California

Sometimes I do what my friends don't want me to do. Then my friends say they won't be my best friend. But I don't worry because tomorrow they're my friends.

Boy, 6, Wyoming

Sometimes I do things so my friends who aren't in my gifted program will like me.

Boy, 10, Georgia

Last year in fifth grade I did something just to go along with the crowd. My parents didn't want me to, but I did. The situation was where no one liked this girl and they made fun of her. I was in with the group that did this, and now I wish I hadn't done it.

Girl, 11, Illinois

I don't go along with the crowd because I think it's wrong to do something that I shouldn't do. If people call me chicken or other names, I just walk away.

Girl, 9, California

My friends and I try to do a little of what each other wants; then we're all happy.

Girl, 7, New York

I don't usually go along with the crowd because I don't usually have a crowd to go along with.

Girl, 11, Maine

I always try to be unique, and if someone asks me to do something just to be popular, I say, "No way!"

Girl, 10, Texas

Sometimes I will go along with the crowd, but I will always keep my own feelings inside.

Girl, 11, Georgia

When I do something that others don't like and I stick by it and see it through, I feel good.

Girl, 11, Georgia

Most of the time I stand up for the things I think are right. Sometimes my friends get mad at me because I don't do what they want, but I don't care because I know what I believe and nothing can change that.

Boy, 11, California

Sometimes when I don't do what people want me to do they get angry with me, but I think that it's my life and I should get to do what *I* want because I'm a person, too.

Girl, 11, California

I used to run with the group, but now I just try to be myself and do my best.

Boy, 12, Ohio

Sometimes I will go along with the crowd. You never know. . . they might be right!

Boy, 10, New York

Speak For Yourself

1. What were some of the reasons kids gave for "going along with the crowd"? What were some of the reasons they gave for *not* doing this?

2. Do you ever just "go along with the crowd"? When is this okay"? When isn't it? Why?

3. Think of a time when you did "go along with the crowd"and felt good about it. Now think of a time when you did and felt not-so-good about it.

4. Think of a time when you didn't "go along with the crowd" and felt good about it. Now think of a time when you didn't go along and felt not-so-good about it.

5. What are some of the consequences of "going along with the crowd" when you don't feel okay about it? What are some things you can say when people try to pressure you into doing what "everyone else" is doing?

CHAPTER 4

◆◆◆◆◆◆◆◆◆◆◆◆◆◆◆◆◆◆◆◆◆◆◆◆◆◆

What's Wrong With School?

◆◆◆◆◆◆◆◆◆◆◆◆◆◆◆◆◆◆◆◆◆◆◆◆◆◆

What Do You Do on a Typical School Day?

I sit there pretending to be reading along when I'm really six pages ahead. Also, when I understand something and half the class doesn't, I have to sit there and listen.

Girl, 11, Illinois

On a regular day-to-day basis we have the same thing over and over.

Boy, 11, New York

We color and we do math. We read about Buffy and Mack. When we are doing work, we cannot get out of our seats except to throw something away. We have to be quiet. We do some more work, then we play, then we have lunch, then we do more work.

Girl, 6, New York

It's a lot of work and I get frustrated. Sometimes I cry when I get home. I hate reading group.

Girl, 8, New York

First, I do morning work. Second, I do my math. Third, I do my Headways book. Fourth, I go to the bathroom. Fifth, I have workshop. Sixth, I go to lunch. Next, I go to recess. Next, I do my reading book. Then I go home. We have only one time to play—that's at recess.

Boy, 9, Connecticut

Most of the time it's just review, review, review.

Girl, 10, Maine

My typical school day is boring. I am lazy and do average. I try to do my work late and I still pass. I take advantage of being gifted.

Girl, 11, New York

Usually, I come to school late, have to fumble at my locker, run up the stairs, and collapse into my seat. Then, it's off to the next class. It's pretty monotonous, but it's a living.

Girl, 13, Connecticut

In a typical school day I whiz through my "extra" classes and plod through the normal ones. Teachers repeat and "go over one more time" and explain until their once-fresh ideas are almost meaningless. At times, I try to block it out and then get reprimanded for not paying attention. Sometimes it's easier to just let the haze creep over my eyes and reply robot-like. But it scares me—sometimes I feel like I'll never come back.

Girl, 12, Connecticut

1. Sleep through reading.
2. Learn in my gifted program.
3. Read through health.
4. Look interested through math.
5. Pretend to take notes through social studies.
6. Throw up during lunch.

Girl, 12, New York

Oh what a bore to sit and listen,
To stuff we already know.
Do everything we've done and done again,
But we still must sit and listen.
Over and over read one more page.
Oh bore,
Oh bore,
Oh bore.
Sometimes I feel if we do one more page
My head will explode with boreness rage
I wish I could get up right there
and march right out the door.

GIRL, 9, NEW YORK

Speak For Yourself

1. What do you do on a typical school day?

2. Do you think you have too much homework or too little? If you could change your school's homework policy, how would you change it?

3. How do you feel about having to review material you already know inside and out? If you could change your school's reviewing policy, how would you change it?

4. If you could do whatever you wanted on a typical school day, what would you do? Which activities would you keep doing? Which would you stop doing? Which new activities would you add to your schedule? Write down your ideas. Then talk them over with your parents. Maybe you and your parents can talk to your teachers—and maybe some of your ideas can be put into action!

What Happens in School That Makes Learning More Difficult or Less Interesting?

Once, in science, my teacher asked a question. I raised my hand to answer but he waved it away saying that he wanted someone other than me to answer because I had been answering too many questions already.

Girl, 11, Michigan

Last year I wasn't at school one day a week (my gifted program was in another school), so I didn't finish all my classwork. I would have finished but my teacher wouldn't let me bring anything home as homework. When my mother asked her about my grade, the teacher said that "if I was smart enough to go to another school I should be smart enough to keep up with my own classwork."

Girl, 10, Connecticut

Most teachers are fair, but some teachers help slower kids get good grades more than brighter ones because they feel if slower kids get bad marks they won't try anymore. Work that would be a D for us might be an A for somebody else. It seems that some students don't work very hard but get better grades than some that do.

Girl, 12, Connecticut

The work isn't challenging a lot of times. Also, when I'm done with my work, I have to wait for other people to finish (especially math).

Boy, 10, Connecticut

Sometimes I get annoyed when teachers have to explain rules and things over and over. So I help other people understand what they have to do. Then we don't have to miss recess.

Girl, 7, New York

There was one instance where I was having trouble finding the correct answer to a question in history. I asked the teacher for help and she refused, saying I was gifted so I should be capable of finding it. This makes me angry, and I've even thought about dropping out of my gifted program.

Girl, 13, Georgia

The teachers often have me do extra things, like move desks or go get their coffee. I think this is indirectly a result of being smart, because I finish my homework first and am sitting there while the others are still writing.

Boy, 12, Ohio

57

I feel sometimes that my teacher is always trying to catch me off guard and that she wants to try to show off my faults. Whenever she plays this game, she always gets mad when I answer correctly.

Girl, 12, Connecticut

I'm not saying that everything should be a production, but teachers should put something of themselves into their lessons.

Girl, 11, Michigan

Most teachers have tried to do something special, but in some grades teachers resented me because there was no one else working on my level. They had to think of extra programs and it was more work for them.

Girl, 11, Connecticut

My math teacher expects me to know how to do very hard problems and won't explain them to me.

Girl, 11, Georgia

If you say, "I don't understand what's going on" they say, "What's not to understand? You should know—you should have been listening." And you *were* listening but you just didn't understand and they won't explain to you. Then, you have a homework paper on that topic and you don't understand what it is all about and as a result you get a bad grade. . . and you want so badly to do well.

Girl, 11, Connecticut

I wish that teachers who use a lot of books would let you write in them. I don't like copying everything from my books onto papers, drawing perfect margins, making a heading, and writing everything exactly right. And. . . if you don't do it exactly the way you are supposed to, you get a "DNFD" which means you did not follow directions, you keep doing it over and over until it is exactly the way the teacher wants it—even if you knew the material before you started.

Girl, 11, Connecticut

I hate it when teachers go into an interesting discussion and then decide that they haven't got time for it. It leaves me in total disappointment. If they didn't have time for it, then they shouldn't have brought it up in the first place!

Boy, 11, Michigan

Speak For Yourself

1. How would *you* answer the question, "What happens in school that makes learning more difficult or less interesting?"

2. Can you think of something a teacher does that bothers you a lot? Talk to your parents about it. Ask them to help you come up with a way to suggest a positive change.

3. Think of something a teacher does that you really like. How could you show this teacher that you appreciate what he or she does for you? Now. . . go do it!

4. Take a long piece of paper (maybe tape several together) and draw a timeline. On one end, write "My birth," and on the other, write "Today." Now fill in important events and occasions that have taken place in your life—both sad and happy events—anything you think was important. When you're through, go back and circle the ones that relate to school. How much of an influence has school had on your life? Parents? Friends? Pets? Other people or things?

Do You Ever Get Bored in School?

School is boring in some subjects because I usually know the answers before the questions are even asked.

Boy, 9, Wyoming

School is Never, I repeat NEVER, EVER boring! It's almost a SIN to say school is boring!

Girl, 10, Illinois

School is boring. Why? I imagine it's because either I know what is being talked about or I can't add anything to what the teacher is saying.

Girl, 11, New York

School is never boring to me. I guess that's because I have a good teacher, or maybe, because if I get bored I know my teacher will give me more work.

Boy, 9, California

The only time that school was ever boring was in my sixth-grade social studies class. I think I was bored because the teacher didn't give us any real challenges. I think, in a way, the teacher *made* it boring.

Girl, 11, New York

I don't think school is boring at all. It's not that it's too difficult or anything, but I work for what I get—it doesn't just come naturally.

Girl, 12, Illinois

School is never boring to me because if I finish my work I always have something to do.

Boy, 10, Wyoming

Yes, when the teacher talks too much.

Girl, 11, New York

Not since I entered seventh grade. In sixth you have the same teacher for six and one half hours. But in seventh you have nine different teachers—and all of them have so many likes and dislikes which are so *unalike*.

Girl, 12, Illinois

I think school work (like writing words five times and putting them into sentences) is as boring as something can be—if you know how to do it already.

Boy, 10, Kansas

School usually doesn't get boring for me, but it's also not my favorite way of spending six and one half hours.

Girl, 11, California

Most of the time I'm bored, because I'd rather play than work.

Girl, 6, New York

Speak For Yourself

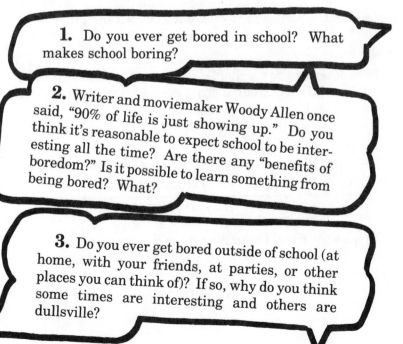

1. Do you ever get bored in school? What makes school boring?

2. Writer and moviemaker Woody Allen once said, "90% of life is just showing up." Do you think it's reasonable to expect school to be interesting all the time? Are there any "benefits of boredom?" Is it possible to learn something from being bored? What?

3. Do you ever get bored outside of school (at home, with your friends, at parties, or other places you can think of)? If so, why do you think some times are interesting and others are dullsville?

When You Get Bored in School, What Do You Do?

I fiddle with my pencils or stare out the window.

> Girl, 8, New York

I sing to myself.

> Boy, 8, New York

What I usually do to get away from a lecture that I could easily give myself is take the bathroom pass even if I don't need it.

> Boy, 9, Wyoming

I imagine things.

> Girl, 9, New York

I just let the day go by. . . it goes by SLOWLY, though.

> Girl, 9, New York

I pretend I'm home watching a rerun of a T.V. show. I remember the scenes in my head and watch the program.

> Girl, 10, New York

To counteract the boredom, I joke around with the people next to me and get in trouble. That makes my recesses boring because then I have to stay inside.

> Boy, 10, Connecticut

I am working to get more creative writing done and to try not to have to do things I already know how to do.

> Boy, 10, Kansas

To pass the time, I usually read or daydream or do something like this paper. I'm answering this question in the middle of a boring class, English.

> Girl, 11, Illinois

To entertain myself, I tap my feet.
Girl, 8, Ohio

Once I told the teacher I was bored and she even admitted that school was boring sometimes. Somehow, that made it seem more bearable.

Girl, 11, Connecticut

I go crazy, absolutely bonkers.

Girl, 11, New York

I like to write stories about my feelings and problems.

Girl, 11, Georgia

I read my favorite magazine.

Boy, 10, New York

When I get bored in math I pretend I am a computer *doing* the math. In social studies I pretend I am one of the people in that country.

Girl, 11, New York

I just cope with it and find out what I can do for extra credit.

Girl, 11, Illinois

I listen as best I can and ask a lot of questions or I think about other things and half-listen so I can answer the teacher's questions.

Girl, 11, New York

I look at all the pictures in the book real close to my face so they look like blurs, and then I pretend they're other things, like an elephant picture turns into a cloud or a lady or anything.

Girl, 11, Puerto Rico

Twice in social studies I fell asleep, but usually I doodle and try to think of how I could learn more in the class even though it is boring. I've come up with a few ideas, like creative projects instead of doing plain old reports, and turning boring assignments into challenges.

Girl, 11, New York

I usually write on my folders or look at the clock every now and then to see how long it takes our teacher to get through the part I already know.

Girl, 12, Illinois

I read a book or try to look interested. (I want to be an actress when I grow up, so this is good practice.)

Girl, 12, New York

I throw down my thoughts on a piece of paper. I'm trying to write a book.

Boy, 12, Connecticut

The teacher I have this year is quite a character. If he starts to get boring, I just watch the way he moves and some of his gestures, which are kind of funny. This keeps me occupied.

Girl, 12, Connecticut

I was in math class last December. Our teacher had given us a long-term assignment and a week to do it in. I finished in on the first day. On the third day I started to get restless, so after counting the math problems left in the chapter, the pages in the chapter, the chapters in the book, and the pages I had already done, I was b*ored*! As a last resort I passed a note saying, "If you don't drop your book at 1:54 you are a purple cow." 1:54 came and everyone dropped their books. The teacher screamed, "Who's responsible for this?"

Girl, 12, Connecticut

Speak For Yourself

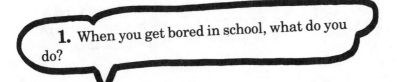

1. When you get bored in school, what do you do?

2. Someone once said, "The cure for boredom is curiosity; there is no cure for curiosity." How can you put your curiosity to work at times when you're bored?

3. Take the letters of the word boring—B-O-R-I-N-G—and use each to start a sentence about something you can do to relieve your boredom. For example.

B: Bake cookies
O: Open a bartering service
R: Read
I: Independent study project
N: Notice something new
G: Grow plants

Keep this list inside your desk and read it whenever you get bored. (Change it occasionally so that if you are bored once in a while you'll have some new ideas ready to go.)

4. If you're tired of (or bored with) doing the same kinds of assignments and projects (book reports, for example) talk with your teachers about doing or making one or more of these:

banners
biographies
blueprints
brochures
cartoons
charts
crossword puzzles
debates
dioramas
experiments
games
graphs
interviews
maps

masks
mobiles
models
mosaics
newspapers
scrapbooks
sculptures
skits
songs
tapes
timelines
and other ideas you can come up with.

CHAPTER 5

◆◆◆◆◆◆◆◆◆◆◆◆◆◆◆◆◆◆◆◆◆◆◆◆◆◆◆◆

What's Right With School?

◆◆◆◆◆◆◆◆◆◆◆◆◆◆◆◆◆◆◆◆◆◆◆◆◆◆◆◆

Describe Your Idea of a "Perfect" School Day

A perfect school day would be having enough work to *fill* the day but not overflow it.

Girl, 11, Michigan

A perfect school day would be when I could come to school and not be called "the smartest kid in the world." But even more important to me would be the day I could come to school and not hear anyone call anybody else a name of any sort. I realize that when the day comes, everyone will be sure of themselves and will not need to put other people down to gain confidence. To go through a day of school with everyone showing love to each other would be a perfect day for me.

Boy, 13, Kentucky

Well, it would be getting straight A's and 100's. And also, the other kids wouldn't laugh at me and stuff. And I could go down to the media center and read.

Girl, 8, New York

If I learned to understand something new in most subjects.

Boy, 12, New York

A perfect school day would be that it would be science day. We would study space, magnets, and computers.

Boy, 10, New York

A perfect school day would be when the sun is shining, everyone is smiling, school work is easy, and we don't have any homework.

Girl, 10, New York

It would be a day that we have an awards assembly. I would *love* it if most of my friends would win awards that I could never win and they would not be mad if *I* won anything.

Girl, 10, Michigan

For a perfect day, all of the kids would be at school; the work would be challenging but fun; the lunch line would be short. At the end of the day I'd have no homework and the bus wouldn't be noisy.

Girl, 10, Michigan

Speak For Yourself

1. Describe your idea of a "perfect" school day.

2. Look back at page 56 and reread your answer to the question, "What do you do on a typical school day?" How does it compare with your answer above?

3. How could you change some of the things you're doing now to make school better for you? How might your ideas for change also help other students in your class?

4. Develop a plan to change something in your school or classroom that might improve things for you—or for other students. Share your plan with your teacher, a counselor, or the principal and ask for their help.

What Makes Learning Fun and Interesting for You?

I enjoy hands-on activities most of all, because they allow you to discover for yourself. Nothing is more strange than finding that all those dull words and figures in your texts actually mean something.

Girl, 12, Connecticut

I really love brainstorming and writing stories and creative thinking books. I don't really like seeing movies and filmstrips—I like movies to entertain me, not teach me.

Girl, 12, Minnesota

Serious problems, like considering every little detail on how to make a town more hospitable.

Boy, 12, New York

I enjoy going on trips so I can really see things. I also like to listen to records or watch a movie to learn things. It's kind of boring to just write our work on paper. I like to really see things and hear things and find out about things all by myself.

Girl, 6, New York

I like making things, not watching things being made.

Boy, 11, Georgia

I like learning by doing experiments and playing math and reading games. It is more fun than only memorizing and doing workbooks.

Girl, 7, New York

I enjoy games that teach, for instance, Scamper. Scamper is a game that teaches children how to use their imaginations. The teacher reads things from a book and we try to imagine the things she says. Sometimes we draw pictures of what we saw in our imaginations. I like to draw the pictures and sometimes the stories are funny.

Girl, 8, Rhode Island

Research. I like to find out new things.

Girl, 9, New York

70

I like classroom discussions. I like them because they give everyone a chance to exchange ideas openly.

Boy, 13, Connecticut

Before, I never used to like book reports, but ever since I did them with Mrs. Foster I've liked them. What she would do is have us either do a news report on it for the class or make costumes and act out our favorite part.

Girl, 10, New York

Field trips and having professionals, scientists, etc. come in and talk to the class.

Girl, 12, Illinois

Calm, quiet teaching. I hate noise and teachers when they yell.

Girl, 7, New York

My fifth-grade teacher makes learning fun by doing an activity to help you learn. We have math sales, and that helps us with money while it's also lots of fun. In studying the Constitution we made bills and voted on them (now we can chew gum in class). For science, when we review for a test we play baseball, boys against girls. The teacher asks a question and if we get it right, that person goes to first base. We study while having fun. I think she is the best teacher I have ever had.

Girl, 10, Connecticut

I like a comical teacher that puts a lot of fun into learning because it makes me want to listen to everything he or she has to say.

Boy, 12, New York

Calligraphy, since now I can do more interesting things for cards. Besides, my handwriting needs all the help it can get!

Girl, 12, Georgia

I like working in groups because if you can't figure out the answer, someone else can.

Boy, 11, New York

I like to be alone with the teacher and work directly with her.

Girl, 11, New York

I most enjoy teaching methods that are *not* logical, where I have a chance to talk or write creatively.

Girl, 11, New York

Speak For Yourself

1. What makes learning fun and interesting for you?

2. What's the best thing that ever happened to you in school? Ask your parents and teachers this question and compare their answers to yours.

3. What's the most important lesson you ever learned in school? Ask your parents and teachers this question and compare their answers to yours.

4. Imagine that you're a college professor. You've been asked to teach a course called "How to Teach Gifted Students." Write a course outline listing learning activities and teaching methods you want your students to use when *they* start teaching gifted kids.

What Could Teachers Do to Make Learning *More* Fun and Interesting for You?

Let us do what we want when we want to.

Girl, 7, Michigan

1. Make sure kids don't hit other kids.
2. Listen to what we say; don't holler as soon as we say one wrong word.
3. Make sure kids don't show off if they get 100.
4. Don't give so much work when the teacher knows we won't be there.
5. Give us short breaks if we have been writing a lot.

Boy, 9, New York

1. It would be nice if I was able to sit alone.
2. If the teacher would not interrupt your work.
3. If the books had some challenge.

Boy, 9, New York

Sometimes I wish I could do woodworking or anything that's unusual.

Girl, 6, New York

1. Have more reading time.
2. Start a foreign language sooner.
3. If you have decided what you want to be, you could start studying that occupation.

Girl, 9, Michigan

Have a science lab table, a planetarium, and an invention room.

Boy, 10, Louisiana

Don't spend the whole period explaining things—just get on with it.

Girl, 10, New York

1. Give us harder work in subjects where we're getting all A's.
2. Don't go on and on about a subject kids already know.
3. Don't sit us near students who want to copy our papers.
4. Don't make us do an assignment that is too easy.
5. Give us extra time in the library.

Girl, 11, Michigan

1. Don't read people's work aloud to the class.
2. Don't say, "There was only one A and so-and-so made it."
3. Don't always call on the smart students to answer harder questions.
4. Don't always expect the smarter people to make better grades than others.

Girl, 11, Kentucky

1. Excelling is allowed.
2. If your work is done you can use the computers.
3. No dwelling on one subject.
4. If you do something right once, you won't have to do it again.
5. Have career lectures.

Boy, 11, Michigan

1. Individualize the work a little so the student could work on things he/she had trouble with.
2. Combine the work with things the students enjoy doing.
3. Give kids more time to voice their opinions.
4. Encourage kids to get involved, to think, to create, to discover.

Girl, 11, New York

1. Expect the best out of the students—no more, no less.
2. Banish all busy work.

Girl, 12, Kentucky

Speak For Yourself

1. What could teachers do to make learning more fun and interesting for you?

2. Write a recipe for "The Perfect Teacher." (Example: Take one part sense of humor, two parts creativity, one part patience, stir well, and bake!)

3. Often it's easiest to remember what you *don't* like about school. Here's an activity that can help you remember what you *do* like about it. Keep a journal for one week. At the end of each day, write down at least one positive thing that happened in school. Then review what you've written at the end of the week. (If you like this activity, do it for a month, two months, or the whole school year.)

4. Think back on all of the teachers you've had. Who was your favorite teacher? Why? What teacher taught you the most? Did you name the same teacher in both cases? Or did you name different teachers? What qualities does a teacher need to be considered among your favorites?

How Should a Gifted Program Be Different from Regular Classes?

We should have more freedom to choose the things we want to study.

Boy, 10, Connecticut

Special projects to learn about famous writers, artists, and dancers would be interesting.

Girl, 8, Illinois

There should be more creative writing and research—doing it! We should be able to work with kids as smart as we are and discuss things like our special problems with being smart.

Boy, 10, Kansas

Instead of just normal work we should have tests every day to see if we are improving. We should get to use materials on our level based on these tests. Every so often we should have a break so we could confer with the teacher regarding what we've done and what we will be doing.

Girl, 8, California

We should have times where kids can study about a subject they want to learn about. We should have trips of special interest for the kids.

Girl, 9, New York

Harder work, tough puzzles, or things that make us think.

Boy, 9, Kansas

We should use computers, play advanced games, and learn a lot about ourselves and how to deal with the fact that other people will always expect more out of us.

Girl, 10, Arkansas

Gifted programs should have special subjects like computers and archeology. I like to go into things that are more sophisticated and complicated.

Boy, 10, Connecticut

I think a gifted program should have challenges, problems to solve, but most important, unstructured methods. For instance, classrooms don't always have to have desks, chairs, and blackboards. Instead, they can have rugs, pillows and discussions.

Girl, 10, Michigan

I think that you should be able to make your own decisions and have an opinion in a gifted program. The school classes don't really give you these opportunities.

Boy, 11, Connecticut

Well, some kids may disagree, but I think we should have more work and harder work. Because what is the use of being gifted if there's nothing to be gifted about?

Girl, 11, Illinois

It should make gifted children feel like they're special. It makes *me* feel special. A gifted program needs a caring teacher that can make a child believe in himself or herself.

Girl, 11, Georgia

A gifted program should have extra stimulating activities. Tailoring to each child would be necessary, too. The program should be fairly upbeat, helping the children like who they are better.

Girl, 12, Connecticut

I don't think we should do more of regular school work in a gifted program. We should go different places and see new things. The program should give us a chance to see and experience new things.

Girl, 12, Illinois

It means fun field trips and having a teacher who isn't so strict that the slightest wrong move warrants a parent/ teacher conference.

Boy, 12, Georgia

Things that kids enjoy, not something that they hate or feel pressured by.

Girl, 11, New York

If you like one subject in your normal class, during your gifted program you should learn more about that subject.

Girl, 11, New York

We should get a chance to express ourselves, be ourselves, and find out who we are. And we do.

Girl, 12, New York

Gifted programs should help kids like me relate to other kids. The programs should provide challenging word and logic problems, and encourage thinking skills. Gifted programs should not go along with the school curriculum, yet help us with our other schoolwork by providing a more extensive knowledge about it. Long-term independent projects are fine, as long as they don't interfere with homework. Most importantly, a gifted program should get kids off their duffs and start them thinking.

Girl, 13, Wyoming

Speak For Yourself

1. How would you answer the question, "How should a gifted program be different from regular classes?"

2. Which subject in your gifted program has been the most interesting? Which has been the least interesting? What were the differences between the two subjects that made one so good and the other so dull?

3. Make a list of daily activities you do in your gifted program. Rate each one on a scale of 1 (blah) to 5 (exciting, terrific, and wonderful). Are there any ways you could turn the 1's into 3's or 5's? Write down your ideas, then talk them over with your parents and teachers. Maybe some of your ideas can be put into action!

What Makes a Teacher a "Gifted Teacher"?

A teacher who does different things is better than a teacher who does the same things every day.

Boy, 8, Massachusetts

When a teacher says nice things about me, gives me the privilege to do something, or says she enjoys helping me at any time, I think she's a gifted teacher for kindness.

Boy, 9, Massachusetts

A Gifted Teacher:

- understands and respects gifted children
- encourages kids to set and achieve high goals
- goes into assignments deeper than the book
- writes compliments on your paper if you did a good job
- is responsible, efficient and smart
- is loving and caring

— BOYS AND GIRLS, 11 AND 12, MICHIGAN

I think a gifted teacher will challenge you and let the sky be your limit. When they go further than the book, it gets people more involved, especially if they bring in their own experiences. A good teacher won't overload you—you'll get breaks when you need them, and you'll get graded firmly but not too strictly.

Boy, 11, Michigan

A gifted teacher should have enough discipline to keep order in a class without being really strict. A gifted teacher should also have ways of teaching that not only the teacher but the majority of students like. She should also push students to their highest extent but know when they are not able to go further.

Boy, 11, West Germany

A gifted teacher opens your mind to help you with your life.

Boy, 11, New Jersey

She treats me like a person, not a little kid! She smiles a lot and understands me and lets me do projects that *I* want to do, no matter how hard they are.

Girl, 12, New York

When I first became involved with the gifted program in school, I was nervous and afraid that my friends would laugh at me. I was afraid that they would think I was "too good for them" and I'd not be accepted into the crowd. I became ashamed of being gifted and at times I felt guilty, as if I had done something wrong. This period of time might have been very frustrating and depressing if it weren't for my gifted teacher. She helped me to realize that being gifted is special, and you should be proud, not ashamed of it. Oh yes, I was still put down, but that didn't matter as long as I had my gifted classes. My whole life centered around them. They were my special place where I could express my opinions and not be laughed at. They were my place of freedom.

Girl, 11, Connecticut

81

Speak For Yourself

1. If you could be Teacher-for-the-Day, what kinds of things would you do?

2. Has one of your teachers been an especially "gifted teacher"? What qualities made him or her stand out from all the rest?

3. How would you answer the question, "What makes a teacher a 'gifted teacher'?"

4. Imagine that your school is interviewing teachers for your gifted program. You have been chosen to help with the interviewing process. You get to ask each candidate three questions. What will your questions be? Why did you choose these questions instead of others?

CHAPTER 6

◆◆◆◆◆◆◆◆◆◆◆◆◆◆◆◆◆◆◆◆◆◆◆◆◆◆◆◆◆◆◆

You And Your Parents

◆◆◆◆◆◆◆◆◆◆◆◆◆◆◆◆◆◆◆◆◆◆◆◆◆◆◆◆◆◆◆

What Have Your Parents Said to You about Being Gifted?

My parents said that because I'm smart I could be anything I want to be when I grow up, from a garbage collector to the president.

Boy, 11, Michigan

My parents say that they are glad I'm smart because I can help the world.

Boy, 7, New York

My parents have talked to me about being smart lots of times. They said I should use my head for doing good and right things. They said I shouldn't be mean to others and that I shouldn't make fun of others because they're not as smart as me. And don't make fun of people and call them stupid because I wouldn't want them to do that to me.

Girl, 9, Massachusetts

They say I am as smart as a computer.

Boy, 9, New York

My parents never talk to me about being smart. I usually don't have any time to talk to my mom. I have to go to practice my piano or go to gymnastics. Sometimes, I just want to play.

Girl, 9, Kentucky

My mom talks to me when I do not want to use my full abilities. For instance, when I want to get out of something because the work is too tough.

Boy, 10, New York

I have gotten three papers this year that had to be signed by my parents because my grade was below 70. My parents say, "For someone with your smarts, that shouldn't have happened."

Girl, 11, Massachusetts

My mom says that I am smart and that I shouldn't try to hide it because it is a fact. She also says I was lucky to be born smart, and now that I have this gift I should use it to the full extent of my abilities.

Girl, 11, Nebraska

They ask me how I feel when other kids tease me about being smart. They give me support.

Girl, 11, Kentucky

My parents have said that I must push myself and set high goals and reach them.

Girl, 11, Michigan

My mother has talked to me about my intelligence and the one thing I remember her telling me was not to think I'm better than anyone else, because I'm not.

Girl, 11, New York

My parents never talk to me about being smart. Most of the time I get the feeling they just don't care.

Girl, 12, Kentucky

My parents talked to me about being smart when I was getting ready to skip fourth grade. They told me that I was gifted and they asked me if I thought I could handle skipping.

Girl, 12, Kentucky

My mother had a long talk with me about it and she told me it was great to be smart but she also told me not to be snobby about it.

Girl, 11, Alaska

Speak For Yourself

1. What have your parents said to you about being gifted?

2. What's one thing you wish your parents would say about you? What's the one thing you wish they would *stop* saying?

3. If you feel comfortable, try talking to your parents about these questions and your answers.

What Do Your Parents Expect from You because You're Gifted?

At home my parents expect me to do things perfectly. For example, when I ask how to spell a word, they ask, "Why are you in the gifted program if you can't spell?"

Girl, 8, Illinois

My mother likes me to improve all the time.

Boy, 9, New York

Parents give you the needed support and put you back on your feet when you're down. My parents don't make a big hullabaloo when I'm not totally an A student. They realize we all have our bad days.

Boy, 11, Michigan

My mother expects me to be smarter than I was before I was labeled "gifted."

Girl, 12, California

I think at home I am expected to be very responsible and I also think my parents get most upset when I bother my brothers. They feel that I am old enough to leave them alone, and they say, "If you're supposed to be so smart and gifted, why don't you act like it?" They really expect me to act grown-up even though I'm still a kid.

Girl, 12, Illinois

I always try to do my best, but for my mom, that isn't enough.

Girl, 12, California

I think that my parents want me to do better at home because I'm gifted. I think they expect too much.

Boy, 10, Kansas

Speak For Yourself

1. Think about these three questions:
- What would you *like* to be doing 15 years from now?
- What do you think you *will* be doing 15 years from now?
- What do you think your parents *expect* you to be doing 15 years from now?

How are your answers similar? How are they different? What do your answers tell you about what you hope to achieve compared with what your parents expect you will do?

2. Do your parents expect more from you because you're gifted? If so, in what ways do they expect more?

3. Do you think your parents' expectations of you would be different if you weren't gifted? Why or why not?

4. What happens when you don't meet your parents' expectations? What do they say or do? How do *you* feel? If you feel comfortable talking to your parents about their expectations, try it. They might not know how you feel.

5. Are your parents' expectations of you too low, too high, or just right? (If their expectations of you are "just right," tell them that, too.)

How Do You Feel When Your Parents Praise You or Brag about You?

When my parents praise me, I feel proud and important.

Boy, 8, Kansas

When my mom or dad say I do well, I feel proud. But when my sister is in the room, I feel sad because no one says anything to her.

Girl, 8, Ohio

When grown-ups praise me around my peers, it makes me sound like I'm the only one with brains.

Boy, 10, Pennsylvania

I get a real good feeling inside me when I know I pleased them.

Girl, 10, Rhode Island

They don't praise me. They always say bad things. My mother sometimes thinks I should be perfect. She only praises my brother, just because he's younger and more gifted than me when *I* was in second grade.

Girl, 10, Maine

When people give me compliments, lots of times I feel embarrassed because I don't know how to react. I don't know whether or not I will sound conceited when I answer them. Lots of times all I do is grin and walk away.

Girl, 10, California

I feel good. I don't say anything like "I know I'm bright." I just say "Thank you" and be done with it.

Girl, 10, Texas

I feel very good all over. I feel like singing.

Boy, 10, Texas

If my parents praise me for being bright in private it really makes me feel good. But when they do it in public it makes me feel a little uncomfortable, and I feel like people will call me "little goody two-shoes."

Boy, 12, Virginia

I feel dumb. I hate when they praise me when one of my friends is around.

Girl, 10, Connecticut

My dad mostly embarrasses me by telling his friends that I'm real smart. I never have the courage to tell him to stop it.

Boy, 11, New York

I like to know people like my work but I'd rather not be praised at all than be embarrassed in front of my friends.

Boy, 11, Massachusetts

When my mother found out I was being put in a gifted program, she called her friends to tell them. Her friends who have children my age told *their* children and all my friends knew before I could tell them. I feel embarrassed telling my mother how I feel about this.

Girl, 11, Connecticut

I don't mind except when my mother brings it into every conversation.

Girl, 11, Alabama

I feel pretty good when I'm by myself and no one thinks I'm spoiled or a teacher's pet, but when I am with other people, I hate being told I am bright because they think I am a bigshot or something.

Girl, 11, Ohio

It's nice when people compliment you, but parents *always* think their children are smart.

Girl, 12, Illinois

I used to think "So what?" but now I really have learned to listen and appreciate compliments and then I tend to put forth more effort. Compliments kind of make me smile— like a hug. They sneak up and surround you to protect you from anything bad.

Girl, 12, Kansas

Speak For Yourself

1. How do you feel when your parents praise you or brag about you?

2. Are there times when their praising or bragging makes you feel good? (For example, when they talk to relatives about you?) Are there times when you wish they would stop? (For example, when your friends are nearby?)

3. If your parents' bragging makes you uncomfortable, they might never know unless you tell them. Think of three ways to let them know how you feel. Try starting each with a positive statement. (Examples: "Dad, I know you're proud of me, but I get embarrassed when you show my report card to the neighbors." Or: "Mom, I'm glad you liked my performance in the school play, but I wish you wouldn't show the pictures to everyone who comes over.") You might be surprised how happy your parents are to hear what you have to say!

Do Your Parents Compare You to Your Brothers and Sisters? How Does That Make You Feel?

I'm compared, by both my parents *and* my brothers. And it makes me feel cruddy.

Girl, 9, Massachusetts

My mother says that I am smarter than my brother. It makes me feel weird. I think he should be smarter than me because he is older.

Boy, 10, West Germany

My mom and dad and other people usually compare me and my sister. They do it by looking at our report cards. And if my sister has a 1 (meaning excellent) and I have a 2 (meaning good) they yell at me, and I don't like that. They make me feel bad.

Girl, 9, New Jersey

I feel my mother thinks my brother's better at games and sports. It makes me feel I'm always the second best at things.

Boy, 9, New York

Sometimes they compare my brother and me and it makes me feel bad because my brother is older than I am and he does things better.

Girl, 9, New York

I have been compared with my sister before. My grand-parents sometimes say to my parents when I'm sitting right there, "My, Martha can do gymnastics so well, why can't Barbara?" That really gets me mad.

Girl, 9, New York

Sometimes my parents say, "Your sister did this and that when she was little, so why can't you?" I feel like saying it's because I'm a different person than my sister!

Girl, 9, Alaska

My step dad compares me to my older step brothers which makes me feel he expects more out of me....Which means they get to do a lot more with Dad than I do (partially because they're boys and I'm not).

Girl, 11, Michigan

I'm compared to my brothers and sisters by my father. It makes me feel like I have to do everything they did—like win spelling bees and science awards.

Girl, 12, Kentucky

My mom *and* dad say that when my older brother was my age he was only 3/4 as smart as me.

Girl, 10, New Jersey

Speak For Yourself

1. Do your parents compare you to your brothers and sisters? How does that make you feel?

2. Sibling rivalry has been around since time began. Brothers and sisters naturally compete with one another. When your parents catch you competing with your siblings, how do they react? Do they encourage the competition? Ignore it? Try to get you to stop competing?

3. What are some ways your parents could encourage you without using comparisons? What could they say or do? List some of your ideas. Then, if you feel comfortable, talk them over with your parents.

4. Do your parents ever compare your brothers and sisters to you? If so, ask your brother or sister how this makes them feel. (If comparisons between family members are a problem, maybe your family could set aside some time to talk about it.)

What Do Your Parents Do to Get You Interested in New Things?

My father teaches me everything in math before I even know what he is talking about. It helps me to really get interested in new topics.

Girl, 10, Massachusetts

My parents have put me in classes that they thought I would like. Also, they take me different places to see things.

Girl, 8, Michigan

My mother and my father got me interested in nature and science because my parents and I go on nature hikes and trails. Learning about nature got a lot of requirements done on my Girl Scout badges, too.

Girl, 9, New York

They have given me responsibility so that I can handle it wisely. They have given me plenty of artistic things, which started my creativity very well.

Boy, 11, Michigan

When my mom wanted me to take ballet, she kept talking about it and then it started to make me curious. She started me in it and now I'm dancing well.

Girl, 11, Massachusetts

My mother took me to the Metropolitan Museum to see the Egyptian exhibition so that I got interested in history.

Boy, 10, New York

My parents get me interested in new topics by encouraging me to read different kind of books. My parents also insist I join things in and out of school to keep busy.

Girl, 11, New York

94

My parents, each in their own way, let me be
independent. I get responsibilities that I can
handle, and I'm very thankful. They treat me like
an adult, talk to me like an adult, and trust me
like an adult. They let me try art, literature
and other special things. And they listen to
me ——it helps so much that they listen. They
let me make decisions for myself, even if they
think it's not a good idea. What's more, they're
very patient -- they help, but they don't push.
Most important, they respect me.

GIRL, II, MICHIGAN

My family has valued education and religion for many generations. When I was small I had many questions to ask about both, and my parents were happy to answer. By asking those questions and getting them answered, I gradually have grown a passion for learning, and all because my parents were there when I needed them.

Girl, 11, Michigan

My parents buy me lots of books, especially books about things I am interested in, like baseball and Greek myths.

Boy, 9, New York

They forced me into it.

Girl, 7, Michigan

If I'm interested in something, they try to find someone who will teach me well!

Girl, 12, New York

Nothing; they don't have to do anything to get me interested in things.

Boy, 8, New York

Speak For Yourself

1. What do your parents do to get you interested in new things?

2. Make a list of activities (both in school and out of school) that you wouldn't be involved in if it hadn't been for your parents. Which activities did they *encourage* you to do? Which did they *force* you to do? Which do you think you'll keep doing on your own when you get older?

3. Make a list of activities (both in school and out of school) that you got involved in on your own, due to your own choosing.

4. Compare the lists you made for Questions 2 and 3. Which activities have been most important to you? Which have been most enjoyable?

5. What's the one thing your parents encouraged (or forced) you to do that you'll always be glad they did?

What Do You Wish Your Parents Would Talk to You About?

Boy-girl relationships, because I'm about ready to have one.

Boy, 10, Michigan

I think they should talk to me more about how they think I am doing in school. It is important to me because then I would know how they feel about it.

Girl, 8, Michigan

The real reason my parents got separated, because I need to know.

Boy, 10, New York

They talk *about* me and where I should go and I think they should talk *to* me to see if I agree on it.

Boy, 9, New York

97

My parents discuss almost everything with me, and what they don't, I usually don't want to know about.

Boy, 11, New York

Speak For Yourself

1. What do you wish your parents would talk to you about?

2. When you want your parents to talk to you about something, do you ask them, or do you wait for them to bring it up? Or do you say nothing at all? Which plan is the most effective? Why?

3. Is there something you need to know about right now? (Something that's really important or something that's been on your mind for a long time.) If you're afraid or embarrassed to ask your parents, try asking your teacher or school counselor. Find out if they have any books or brochures on the subject that you can take home and maybe share with your parents. Most teachers and counselors are glad to help if they can and won't think your question is "stupid" or "silly."

What Makes You Happiest at Home?

When we have all the time in the world.

Boy, 8, New York

When my grandma, grandpa, aunt and uncle come over and we all laugh, tell each other our latest jokes, and eat dinner.

Girl, 10, Michigan

When I cuddle with my mother.

Girl, 8, New York

When I am alone with one of my parents and we are having a nice, quiet time.

Girl, 9, Ohio

When my father takes time with me on things I want to learn. He shows me he loves me, tries to teach me.

Boy, 9, Massachusetts

My mom is a counselor and she is sensitive and listens to my problems. She is there any time I need her.

Girl, 10, Louisiana

My dad spends a lot of time with me on the weekends, playing games and sports with me. He coaches basketball and baseball and has taught me all the sports I know how to play. I have learned to make friends easily. Even though I am bright, he has made me feel like a "regular American kid."

Boy, 11, New Jersey

I'm probably happiest at home when I have a bad day at school and I walk inside my home and my mom gives me a kiss promptly.

Boy, 11, Louisiana

I'm happiest at home when our whole family is sitting around the quartz heater together, and when we are playing ping-pong.

Boy, 11, Minnesota

Speak For Yourself

1. What makes you happiest at home?

2. What are some things you and your parents do together that you really enjoy? Think of a special way to say "thank you" for the good times you have together.

3. Are there other things you would like to do with your parents? Make a list, then talk things over with them. Maybe they can make up a "wish list," too. That way you can find out what their idea of a good time with you is!

CHAPTER 7

‹‹‹‹‹‹‹‹‹‹‹‹‹‹‹‹‹‹‹‹‹‹‹‹‹‹‹‹

Looking Ahead

‹‹‹‹‹‹‹‹‹‹‹‹‹‹‹‹‹‹‹‹‹‹‹‹‹‹‹‹

What Would You Like to Learn about Someday?

I would want to study stars. Sometime, I want to sleep in a tent and in the night go outside and find the Big Dipper and other constellations.

> Girl, 8, New York

This isn't a school subject, but I'd like to study about *people* so that if they have problems, I can help them.

> Girl, 9, Massachusetts

I would like to learn about John Alden because I know one of his descendants.

> Girl, 9, Connecticut

I would like to learn how to make a book—binding, covering, writing, the whole thing. I plan to write books and if I learn how to do these things, I could give someone a book that I had made all by myself.

> Girl, 10, Kentucky

Amelia Earhart. I want to find out where she crashed and how. I've always liked her, but I'm not sure why.

Girl, 9, Kentucky

I think I would like to learn about Easter Island because I like archeology.

Girl, 9, Kentucky

I would like to study about computers and work with them because someday everything will be run by a computer and so I would like to work with them now so that I have a little head start.

Girl, 10, New York

I would like to learn about and work with chemicals. It is neat how acids can burn holes in things.

Girl, 10, Michigan

I would like to learn about space travel because it seems to be the ultimate thing these days.

Boy, 11, Massachusetts

I would like to study fossils because they're so interesting. For instance, sometimes worms will leave marks in rocks and it's kind of weird because worms don't seem heavy enough to leave trails. I like fossils because they're like preservatives and they save bones and tracks made a long time ago.

Girl, 10, New York

I'd like to learn about records. I'd like to know how sound gets into the grooves and is able to come out in the form of music.

Girl, 11, Massachusetts

I have always wanted to know how the eye works—how it gives you a picture.

Girl, 11, Michigan

I think I would like to study more about prehistoric times. I'm interested in how the dinosaurs suddenly "disappeared." There are a few very possible explanations, but there really isn't a lot of proof that any are true.

Girl, 11, New York

I would like to learn more about Catholics. My mother is Methodist, so that's our religion. But I don't know much info on other religions so I want to have more.

Girl, 11, Louisiana

Medieval weaponry, because that way I will know what a weapon looks like when I play *Dungeons and Dragons*.

Boy, 11, Minnesota

I would like to study about animal behavior because I *love* animals and I would like to be with them all my life. I would also like to know how to help them not become extinct.

Girl, 12, New York

Speak For Yourself

1. What would you like to learn about someday?

2. You don't have to wait until "someday" to start learning about what interests you. There are many people around who can help—your parents, your teachers, librarians, and other adults in your community. Often a public or school library will have a "Community Resource File" listing names and telephone numbers of local experts or specialists who are willing to share their time and knowledge. Ask!

What Are Your Plans
for the Future?

I want to be a surgeon because I want to learn how the insides of people work.

Boy, 10, West Germany

I will go to high school, and for college, I will go to the University of Florida. Then I'll become a real estator or get involved in computers. I might get married and then go into retirement and Medicare.

Boy, 10, Kentucky

To either teach children that are mentally handicapped or (most probably) go to hospitals and dance and sing for them.

Girl, 9, Massachusetts

My future plans are to go to Penn State and play either football or baseball or both. And whichever one I like best will be my career. I will also take up some kind of back-up career, like law.

Boy, 10, Alaska

I would like to become a professor or a scientist. I think I would like to create things that would help the world. It would also be interesting to pass on the information I have learned to others.

Boy, 10, New York

1. Go to college and graduate school.
2. Get married and find a well-paying job.
3. Help my children to become good people.

Girl, 10, New York

I'd like to be an actress, singer, physical therapist, or teacher. When I'm about 20, I plan to pursue my career (whatever it is) and find the perfect place to live and work.

Girl, 10, Connecticut

When I grow up I'll have a mustache, a Fiat, and I'll be a naturalist and I'll adopt twins.

Boy, 11, Michigan

When I retire I would like to travel around to China, Africa, and other places I would enjoy seeing. After that, I would like to find a nice, cozy house to live in in Switzerland.

Girl, 10, Michigan

I want to grow up to be a professional ballet dancer. I want to do archeology in my spare time. I plan to be single and travel around the world.

Girl, 11, Michigan

I might be a child psychiatrist. I am very interested in exploring the mind and I also want to help other people (which will make me feel more useful to the world).

Girl, 11, Louisiana

I plant to be an architect. I'm already drawing plans.

Boy, 11, Louisiana

To become a pro football player and not to sit on the bench all the time.

Boy, 11, Louisiana

Most kids want to be doctors, lawyers, or artists, but I want to be an athlete of some kind.

Boy, 11, Georgia

I'm not sure. But I really would love to be a detective. Everybody laughs when I tell them this, but I am interested in that subject and I just might grow up and make it work.

Girl, 12, Michigan

I would like to be an Egyptologist or doctor. I *really* couldn't see myself as a secretary.

Girl, 11, Massachusetts

My future plans were to be a teacher, but my mom said that with my brains I should be something else.

Girl, 12, Michigan

In our school we have what's called "group guidance." This is a course that helps you to choose a career and set values for what you think is most important so you will choose a good career for you and your lifestyle. Ever since I was little I've wanted to be a lawyer because I think that some things that are in laws should be changed. I also plan to achieve high in my high school so I will be able to attend Harvard College and Law School. In the way, way future, I plan to become president of the U.S. or a senator or congressman so I can change things that aren't fair to someone or a group of people.

Girl, 13, New Jersey

I want to be a mom and a waitress and a lawyer.

Girl, 6, Michigan

I want to go to college and be a half-time ski instructor.

Girl, 8, Michigan

I would like to be a veterinarian because I love pets and if they were sick or needed shots I would be glad to help them. I know how it feels to have a pet die or run away. One cat of mine went hunting one day and never came back.

Girl, 9, New York

I had two plans for my career. One was to be a dancer and the other was to be a teacher. So I decided to be a dance teacher.

Girl, 8, New York

My future plans are to grow up and try to work hard to be a dentist. I'd like to be a dentist because it seems a little challenging to find out if anybody has cavities. I wouldn't charge much of a fee. I'm thinking about retiring at 54.

Boy, 9, New York

I plan to finish college and get a teaching degree and teach kids with problems or a gifted class. After I retire, I plan to write stories. (I love to write!) Those are my only plans if I don't succeed in my first wish: I want to be the first woman president.

Girl, 10, Kentucky

I plan to be a doctor. I think I'll get married someday and maybe have a few kids. In my spare time, I'll write poetry.

Girl, 10, Michigan

I don't want to be noticed as being smart. I just want to be a regular housewife because I don't think it's fair that just because I'm smart I have to be a scientist or something.

Girl, 10, New York

A lot of things—go to college, ride horses, learn about people, and fly to the stars.

Girl, 6, Massachusetts

Speak For Yourself

1. What are your plans for the future?

2. What do you think it will be like to be grown-up, living away from your parents, and working? Close your eyes and try to imagine what you might look like. . . where you might live. . . what kinds of friends you might have. . . what your job might be. . . what you might do for fun. Write down what you "see" for your future.

3. Learn about three careers you don't know anything about. Start by looking through the contents in your local Yellow Pages telephone directory. You'll find professions that seem funny (like "Rubber Consultant"), mysterious (like "Exodontist"), or just plain interesting (like "Beach Pollution Controller"). You may want to ask your teacher for a special assignment to explore those you chose. Then call someone listed under each heading in the Yellow Pages and ask him or her to describe that profession. Report back to the class on what you learned.

4. Forty years ago, there were no computer programmers, astronauts, laser photographers, or solar energy technicians—just to name a few "new" careers. Can you imagine a job that doesn't exist today but might in 20 or 40 years from today? Describe the job and name some of the qualifications a person interested in it might need.

5. Can you think of a job that exists today but might not exist in the not too distant future? What are some of the reasons for your "projection"?

6. Can you think of a job that will probably never be out of date? Why will this job always be available?

7. After completing Questions 1-6, decide which job or career you'd like to have as an adult. Why would you choose this occupation over the thousands of others that will probably be available?

Appendix

Resources for Grown-ups

If your parents or teachers want to know more about giftedness, here are some resources we recommend.

Giftedness, Conflict, and Underachievement by Joanne Rand Whitmore. Allyn and Bacon, Boston, MA, 1980. 462 pages.

This textbook provides proof that the phenomenon of underachievement in gifted children is neither totally debilitating nor irreversible. Using case studies and research, the author explains underlying causes of academic and social maladjustment. Next, she reviews methods for reversing underachievement through strategies that can be implemented by classroom teachers or teachers of the gifted. A thorough review of research studies in self-concept/self-esteem and gifted child education is also included.

Inviting School Success: A Self-Concept Approach to Teaching and Learning by William Watson Purkey and John M. Novak. Wadsworth Publishers, Belmont, CA, 1984. 159 pages.

Everything a teacher does—every smile and frown, laugh and yell, instruction given and grade recorded—is either an invitation or a "disinvitation" to learn. Students are keen to these cues, and in his short book, Purkey points out ways that teachers can attend to the subtle messages they send to pupils through their comments, actions, and reactions.

Roeper Review: A Journal on Gifted Education, P.O. Box 329, Bloomfield Hills, MI 48013.

A quarterly journal devoted to gifted child education, *Roeper Review* is the most comprehensive periodical available for persons interested in current trends and research involving gifted children. Each issue has two theme sections (for example, "Pre-School Giftedness" or "The Learning Disabled Gifted Child") containing articles written by leading educational researchers or practitioners. Also, there are numerous reviews of curriculum materials, gifted program descriptions, a summary of recent doctoral research in gifted child education, and a special section for parents of gifted children.

Parents' Guide to Raising a Gifted Child by the *Gifted Children Monthly* Editors and James Alvino. Ballantine, 1986.

The subtitle of this book, "Recognizing and Developing Your Child's Potential," says it all. Every aspect of a gifted child's development—intellectual, social, emotional, physical—is addressed in this volume. The advice given in this book is very practical and positive and will be appreciated by parents of all gifted children.

The Bookfinder (3rd edition) by Sharon Spredmann Dreyer. American Guidance Service, Circle Pines, MN, 1985. 521 pages.

This reference book lists and annotates 725 children's books published from 1979-1982. Expertly edited and cross-referenced, this volume will help you locate books on any of a number of topics—from "name-calling" to "moving to a new town" to "divorce." A superb resource that is reissued every few years, each *Bookfinder* edition lists different books. You need look no further than this book to begin collecting purposeful and enjoyable books for your home or school library.